UNITY
LIBERTY
a n d
CHARITY

*Building Bridges
Under Icy Waters*

DONALD E. MESSER
a n d
WILLIAM J. ABRAHAM
e d i t o r s

ABINGDON PRESS
Nashville

To

Mark, Alan, Debra, Tiffany, Jason, Brad, Rick, and Angie Nagel

and

The Reverend Dr. Dennis Cooke

UNITY, LIBERTY, AND CHARITY:
BUILDING BRIDGES UNDER ICY WATERS

Copyright © 1996 by Abingdon Press

This book is printed on recycled, acid-free paper.

Library of Congress Cataloging-in-Publication Data

Unity, liberty, and charity : building bridges under icy waters /
   edited by Donald E. Messer and William J. Abraham.
      p.   cm.
   Includes bibliographical references and index.
   ISBN 0-687-03306-3 (pbk. :   alk. paper)
     1. United Methodist Church (U.S.)—Doctrines.   2. Church
controversies—United Methodist Church (U.S.)   3. United Methodist
Church (U.S.)—Membership.   4. United Methodist Church (U.S.)—
History—20th century.   5. Methodist Church—United States—
History.   I. Messer, Donald E.   II. Abraham, William J. (William
James), 1947–
BX8331.2.U55   1996
287'.6—dc20   96-11266
                                           CIP

96 97 98 99 00 01 02 03 04 05 —10 9 8 7 6 5 4 3 2 1

MANUFACTURED IN THE UNITED STATES OF AMERICA

CONTENTS

ACKNOWLEDGMENTS

Concerned with growing polarization and politicalization within our beloved church, the editors have sought to encourage and participate in open theological conversations where persons of deep and diverse convictions could articulate their differences and explore possible convergences in thought and action.

The idea of this book emerged from meeting several times with a divergent group of so-called evangelicals and liberals, who call themselves United Methodist Dialogue. When the committee responsible for the 1996 General Conference accepted Dialogue's proposal that the Conference's theme be "in essentials, unity; in non-essentials, liberty; and, in all things, charity," we were assigned the task of encouraging essays around this general epigram. In the process, we went a step further than earlier envisioned, and with the encouragement and support of Abingdon Press developed this study book for individuals and church groups.

Thus this volume does not pretend to reflect or record the spirit and discussions of United Methodist Dialogue. Not all the invited authors have been participants in this circle, though all embrace the concept of attempting to build bridges under the often icy waters separating "evangelicals" and "liberals." Likewise, due to both space limitations and the need to be more inclusive, not everyone in Dialogue contributed essays. Even so, we do not presume to have included all the various viewpoints representative of contemporary laity and clergy within our denomination.

Among the many values of meeting with United Methodist Dialogue has been for us to experience the truth expressed by an African theologian: "Enlargement of love is only possible when there is enlargement of acquaintance."[1] With special gratitude we acknowledge our indebtedness to the following sisters and brothers who have met together with us at various times under the umbrella of United Methodist Dialogue: Gilbert Caldwell, Riley Case, Maxie Dunnam, Sally Geis, William Hinson, James Jackson, Charlene Kammerer, Evelyn Laycock, Robin Lovin, Joy Moore, Harriett Olson, William K. Quick, Randy Smith, and Mark Trotter.

Another value has been for us as editors to become better acquainted. Until this book project suddenly emerged, our relationships have been quite limited. Unfortunately, relatively few models exist of "evangelical" and "liberal" authors working together. We hope that coediting this manuscript may encourage other expressions of cooperation at the parish and seminary levels.

Special thanks also needs to be extended to those who accepted the challenge of writing chapters for this book. Under exceptionally tight timetables, they manifested not only great talent but considerable sacrifice to meet deadlines. They, of course, are responsible for their contributions, but final editing decisions rest with us.

Both of us are especially indebted to Alberta Smith at the Iliff School of Theology, who supervised the many details necessary for publication, including final preparation of the manuscript. William J. Abraham expresses special appreciation for assistance he received during this publication process from Cornelia DeLee, Chuck Gutenson, and Muriel E. Abraham. Donald E. Messer acknowledges deep gratitude to Delwin Brown, Gene Crytzer, Revel Loedy, Bonnie J. Messer, Kama Morton, and Shannon Kimbell-Auth, along with extra-special thanks to Gary and JoAnn Oakley for writing at their home in Kauai, Hawaii.

Additionally, we note our thankfulness for the support of our theological schools: Perkins School of Theology, Southern Methodist University, Dallas, Texas, where Billy is the Albert Cook Outler Professor of Wesley Studies, and the Iliff School of Theology, in Denver, Colorado, where Don is president and Henry White Warren Professor of Practical Theology.

NOTE

1. Anonymous quotation in *Global Challenges,* Association of Theological Schools, June 16-18, 1986, p. 67.

CONTRIBUTORS

William J. Abraham, Dallas, Texas, was born and raised in Northern Ireland and ordained in the Irish Methodist Church. He earned his doctorate at the University of Oxford. Since 1985 he has taught at Perkins School of Theology, where he serves as Albert Cook Outler Professor of Wesley Studies. His books include *Waking from Doctrinal Amnesia, Divine Revelation and the Limits of Historical Criticism,* and *The Logic of Evangelism.* Currently he is engaged in extensive research on the issues of authority and divine agency. He travels extensively as a preacher and lecturer.

Maxie D. Dunnam, president of Asbury Theological Seminary, Wilmore, Kentucky, previously served as Senior Minister of Christ United Methodist Church in Memphis, Tennessee, and World Editor of The Upper Room. Author of many books, his most recent include *The Workbook on Loving the Jesus Way, This Is Christianity,* and *Pack Up Your Troubles: Sermons on How to Trust in God.* He chairs World Evangelism of the World Methodist Council, the World Methodist Evangelism Institute, and has been honored by the Foundation for Evangelism as one of Forty Distinguished Evangelists of the Methodist world in this century. He serves on the General Board of Higher Education and Ministry.

Justo L. González, Decatur, Georgia, retired member of the Rio Grande Conference, previously taught church history and historical theology before devoting full time to writing, editing, and lecturing. He is Executive Director of the Hispanic Theological Initiative and Director of the Hispanic Summer Program. He edits the fourteen-volume Spanish edition of the *Works of John Wesley.*

His most recent book is *Santa Biblia: Reading the Bible Through Hispanic Eyes*. He also serves as editor of the journal *Apuntes*.

S. Michael Hahm currently serves as Executive Secretary for Asia/Pacific and Global Justice Ministries at the United Methodist General Board of Global Ministries in New York, New York. He earned his Ph.D. at Boston University and is a member of the New England Conference. He served as the Dean of the United Graduate University, Yonsei University, Seoul, Korea, 1970–1975. He serves on a variety of ecumenical and social justice boards and agencies, and has been called upon by the Mayor of New York to mediate interethnic conflicts in the community.

Richard P. Heitzenrater is Professor of Church History and Wesley Studies at the Divinity School, Duke University, in Durham, North Carolina. Best known for "breaking the code" of Wesley's diaries, he presently serves as General Editor of the *Bicentennial Edition of the Works of John Wesley*. He has published a dozen books, including *Wesley and the People Called Methodists, The Elusive Mr. Wesley,* and several volumes of Wesley's *Journals & Diaries*. He chaired the writing committee that wrote the doctrinal statement in Part II of *The Book of Discipline*.

Rosemary Skinner Keller is Vice President and Dean of Academic Affairs, and Professor of Religion and American Culture, at Garrett-Evangelical Theological Seminary in Evanston, Illinois. Her publications include *Georgia Harkness: For Such a Time As This, Patriotism and the Female Sex: Abigail Adams and the American Revolution,* and *Spirituality and Social Responsibility: Vocational Vision of Women in the United Methodist Tradition.* She served as a director of the United Methodist General Commission on Christian Unity and Interreligious Concerns (1992–1996).

Donald E. Messer serves as President and Henry White Warren Professor of Practical Theology at The Iliff School of Theology in Denver, Colorado. His seven books include *Christian Ethics and Political Action, Contemporary Images of Christian Ministry, A Conspiracy of Goodness, Calling Church and Seminary into the 21st Century,* and *Caught in the Crossfire: Helping Christians Debate Homosexuality* (coeditor). He has been elected to four General

8

Conferences and serves as a director of the General Board of Global Ministries.

Ruediger R. Minor is episcopal leader of the Eurasia Area of The United Methodist Church. He resides in Moscow, Russia. A native of Leipzig, Germany, he studied theology at United Methodist Theological Seminary Bad Klosterlausnitz in the former East Germany and received a Ph.D. in Church History from Leipzig University. He joined the East German Annual Conference and was ordained an elder in 1966. He was a faculty member and dean at the United Methodist Seminary Bad Klosterlausnitz in former East Germany, and has served several churches in Germany prior to his election to the episcopacy in 1986. He was elected bishop of the Eurasia Area in 1993.

Joy J. Moore is pastor of the United Methodist Church in Battle Creek, Michigan. A graduate of Garrett-Evangelical Theological School and member of the West Michigan Annual Conference, she is a delegate to the 1996 General and Jurisdictional Conferences. She served as campus minister at Adrian College and is active in the "Confessing Movement" of The United Methodist Church.

Harriett J. Olson is an active member of the United Methodist Church on the Green in Morristown, New Jersey, where she assists in youth activities, the partner church relationship with a congregation in Ukraine and United Methodist Women. She is also a partner in a large New Jersey law firm, practicing real estate and environmental law. In addition, she chairs the Northern New Jersey Council on Ministries and is a member and chair of the Finance Committee of the General Board of Discipleship. She has a B.A. from Houghton College and a J.D. from the Harvard Law School.

Marjorie Hewitt Suchocki is Vice President for Academic Affairs and Dean at the School of Theology at Claremont, where she is also the Ingraham Professor of Religion. Her five books include *In God's Presence: Theological Reflections on Prayer, The Fall to Violence: Original Sin in Relational Theology,* and *God Christ Church: A Practical Guide to Process Theology.* She has served on the University Senate of The United Methodist Church, and chaired the Commission on Theological Education.

Mark Trotter has been Senior Minister of the First United Methodist Church, San Diego, California, since 1976. Prior to that he served parishes in Anaheim and Pasadena, California. He has been a delegate to General Conference of the United Methodist Church five times. Since 1988, he has served as a Director on the General Board of Discipleship. He was chairperson of the Committee to Study Baptism, which produced the document, "By Water and the Spirit," for the 1968 General Conference. He is the author of three books: *Grace All The Way Home, You Haven't Seen Anything Yet,* and *What Are You Waiting For?*

Jerry L. Walls has taught philosophy of religion at Asbury Seminary since 1987. An Ordained Elder in the West Ohio Conference, he pastored three years before doing his Ph.D. in philosophy at Notre Dame. Professional affiliations include the American Philosophical Association, and his spiritual autobiography was recently published in *God and the Philosophers.* Among his other publications are two books: *The Problem of Pluralism: Recovering United Methodist Identity,* and *Hell: The Logic of Damnation.* He has also published several poems and won first place in the poetry division in the Christianity and Literature writing contest as an undergraduate.

INTRODUCTION

Building Bridges Under Icy Waters
Donald E. Messer

Division and disunity threaten the future of United Methodism. Especially evident is the split between so-called evangelicals and liberals, which at times seems to portend schism.[1]

Sociologist James Davison Hunter has suggested similar cleavages in American culture, which originate in competing moral visions based on fundamentally different assumptions about moral authority that "are rooted in religious traditions and address our core beliefs about what is right and wrong, good and bad, acceptable and unacceptable in our private and public lives."[2] These competing perspectives are not always clearly coherent or plainly articulated, but they function as polarizing dispositions in our thinking. Hunter identifies these differences as "the impulse toward orthodoxy and the impulse toward progressivism." Generally, the orthodox, or more conservative, position asserts that moral laws by which we live are eternal and unchanging. In contrast, the progressivist, or more liberal, posture presumes truth is not fixed forever, but an unfolding revelation based on our knowledge and experience of the world in relation to Scripture.[3]

This division has emerged with intensity among all the mainline denominations. National studies reveal that the "population divides itself almost evenly between these two categories, with various gradations of extremity and moderation in each. . . . Lutherans, Baptists, Methodists, and Roman Catholics all have about equal numbers of religious liberals and religious conservatives among their members."[4]

Though the vast majority of church members probably don't identify with either label, and compose a vital center majority, all

11

are touched by the struggle of competing theological and political forces within the church and society.[5]

Even defining what it means to be a "liberal" or "conservative" can be problematic and sometimes polemical. Woodrow Wilson once described a conservative as a person "who just sits and thinks, mostly sits." Robert Frost suggested a liberal is a person "too broadminded to take his own side in a quarrel."[6] Moving beyond such stereotyping, this book does not attempt a precise definition of terms, but allows persons to identify themselves along the "conservative/liberal" or "evangelical/progressivist" continuum. The editors, William J. Abraham and I, would describe ourselves as "evangelical" and "liberal," respectively. Likewise, the other authors represented in this book fall basically, though not narrowly, into these general categories.

Speaking Ill of Our Sisters and Brothers

For centuries Christians saw themselves in competition with others, Catholics versus Protestants versus Jews. In my youth it was customary to criticize persons of other denominations and to claim superiority for one's own faith community. I remember in my small hometown church in Kimball, South Dakota, people saying they wouldn't want to share their hymnals with the Presbyterians. Certainly we didn't approve the behavior of the Catholics playing bingo. The success of the ecumenical movement has been evidenced by the overcoming of these petty prejudices and a deepening of religious ties. Now for more than twenty-five years in my small rural town Lutherans, Presbyterians, and United Methodists have been sharing a common pastor, worshiping and working together, while maintaining their denominational identity. After Vatican II, my parents began playing cards on Sunday night in the Roman Catholic parish hall. When my father died, the Catholic priest came to his funeral—the first time anyone in that small community had ever seen a Catholic priest at a Protestant's funeral.

Ironically, with those walls of hostility crumbling, Christians within the same denomination now have considerable difficulty communicating with one another. Pogo's familiar comment takes on new meaning: "We have met the enemy and he is us!" That "us" rarely proves to be some person of another religious persuasion, but more likely is one of our own who bears the name of United Methodist. The "good news/bad news" scenario means we are less likely to criticize other denominational doctrines or policies or leaders; rather we vilify our own sisters and brothers and our own beloved institutions!

Too often, Robert Wuthnow reports, "liberals look across the theological fence at their conservative cousins and see rigid, narrow-minded, moralistic fanatics; while conservatives holler back with taunts that liberals are immoral, loose, biblically illiterate, and unsaved."[7] This split within our denominations becomes politicized by various groups and caucuses ready to do battle on seemingly every issue at our state and national conferences, leading many to fear greater divisions in the near future.

Political elections in the United States tend to heighten the division between Christians. "Us" versus "them" within Protestantism has been heightened by the strong emergence of the religious right. Liberals of any sort—religious or political—have become a "demonized enemy" to the Christian right.[8] Liberals express similar feelings of antipathy toward conservative Christians.

As the denomination declines in membership and influence in the society, internal bickering, and even name-calling, seems to be increasing. Theological polarization and politicalization often negate our witness and paralyze our work in the name of Jesus Christ.

In a world where the forces of evil are everywhere evident and the powers of good seem terribly limited, the divided and sometimes contentious character of our churches must be scandalous in the eyes of God and many persons of goodwill. For "if one views the situation from the standpoint of Christian principles," says Robert Wuthnow,

one can only decry the ill will, the absence of brotherly and sisterly love, and the prevalence of dogmatism and bigotry that characterize present relations between conservative and liberal Christians. Scholars on both sides who care about the Christian virtues of harmony and reconciliation could clearly take a more active role in understanding and helping to mitigate these conflicts.[9]

This book represents a manifestation of our rejection of ill will and expresses our care for the Christian virtues of harmony and reconciliation.

Amigos por Jesús

An appropriate scriptural beginning point for building bridges between liberals and conservatives appears in John 15:1-17. "I am the true vine, and my Father is the vinegrower. . . . I am the vine, you are the branches. Those who abide in me and I in them bear much fruit, because apart from me you can do nothing" (vv. 1, 5). Jesus utilizes the metaphor of the vine and branches, linking discipleship with mutual love. As the *Harper Bible Commentary* notes, "the awful consequence of not abiding in Jesus' love by expressing love for one's fellow disciple is made clear by the imagery of casting out (as distinguished from pruning) and burn-ing (vv. 2, 6)."[10] Communion with God means life together as loving friends in Christ.

The vision set forth by Jesus in this passage presumes that Christians will love one another. "This is my commandment, that you love one another as I have loved you" (v. 12). We are charged to be friends. Like the words on a T-shirt that I saw a boy wearing in Argentina, we are called to be *"amigos por Jesús."* We have been appointed disciples, "friends for Jesus," so we can bear fruit by loving one another. For, as Jesus commanded, just before his crucifixion, "By this everyone will know that you are my disciples, if you have love for one another" (John 13:35).

When I compare these teachings of Jesus with the current, almost warlike political conditions within many of our churches, I am tempted to despair. How can we hope to share the bread of Jesus' love to a spiritually hungry world if we can't break through the alienation and anger within our own denomination? How can we hope to evangelize the world for Jesus if we speak ill of our own sisters and brothers? How can we teach the love of neighbors and enemies if we can't tolerate those already within the household of faith? How can we hope to respond to Christ's call for unity, when we seem to be intent on multiplying our divisions?

Unless we create bridges of mutual understanding, respect, and appreciation, then like suicidal lemmings crashing over the cliff, we will self-destruct. And we will have failed to follow Jesus' command: ". . . love one another as I have loved you. No one has greater love than this, to lay down one's life for one's friends" (John 15:12-13).

Bridge Building: Pivotal to Ministry

Bridge building is pivotal to Christian ministry. The very word for priest in Latin is *pontifex,* meaning "bridge builder."[Historically the church at its best has sought to create connections between peoples and between God and humanity.[11]]

A true story emerging from World War II could become a parable for our mission and ministry. During World War II the Russian soldiers at the Rzhev front grumbled and cursed when their commander ordered them to build a bridge across a nearby river. How could they build a bridge when the Nazis on the other side were watching? Once they saw it being built, would they not destroy it?

Engineer Sosnovkin designed the bridge to be built in sections, eighteen inches below the surface of the icy waters. The Russians had to practice underwater construction on their side of the river, in places where the Germans could not see what was happening. This meant setting log pillars solidly in stone foundations and clamping crosspieces to pillars with oiled nuts and bolts. Working in the darkness and freezing waters, they had to learn to do all this by touch.

Since the Russian side of the river was very visible, and the German side had a high bank, the decision was made to build the bridge backwards. When darkness covered the moon and snow shrouded the river, the strongest Russian swimmers dared to cross over with foundation stones on stretchers and in their tunics. Other Russians swam with logs. In the eerie silence, and blue-black with cold, they built the first section of the bridge. Working chest-deep in the freezing waters near the Nazi soldiers, their bodies were bloodied by the ice floes. At one point, the Germans, hearing noises, shot randomly toward the river, wounding several Russians. But the work continued night after night, as they built a secret bridge under the river's surface:

Then one morning, engineer Sosnovkin placed small stakes on the thin ice to mark the location of the bridge. As he waited and watched, the Russian artillery suddenly started firing at the other side and the Nazis returned the shelling. To the utter shock of the German army, Russian tanks, whitened for winter war, came charging down the bank, crashing through the thin ice, and storming across the river on the hidden bridge. Squadron after squadron roared across toward the stupefied Nazis, opening the Rzhev offensive.[12]

As a person committed to nonviolence, I always hesitate to use war stories, but I think we can transform this into a metaphor of building hidden bridges under icy waters. Let us construct bridges, not in order to assault others, but to create needed spans of understanding and communication. Perhaps we could even paraphrase Simon and Garfunkel and sing "Bridge *Under* Troubled Waters"!

Abridging Our Differences

Various efforts are under way around the globe to abridge the differences that scandalize the faith and scuttle the mission of the church in the world today. A series of encounters between the World Council of Churches and evangelical churches have been planned. The first was held during 1993 in Quito, Ecuador, at a Catholic retreat center. Since the last World Council Assembly in Canberra, Australia, in 1991, a number of meetings have occurred between the staff of the WCC and two large evangelical bodies (the World Evangelical Fellowship and World Vision). The primary goal of these meetings has been "to bridge the historic divide which often prevents 'evangelicals' and 'ecumenists' from even talking to each other, allowing ignorance and stereotypes to flourish on both sides."[13]

Dialogue between representatives of the National Council of Churches and evangelical groups has also occurred. The most publicized was when world-renowned evangelist Billy Graham visited the headquarters of the NCC to dialogue with its General

Secretary, Joan Brown Campbell. Roman Catholics and evangelicals have recently joined together in signing a document entitled
"Evangelicals and Catholics Together." Their intent was primarily
to reinforce common convictions and values on certain social
issues as they sought to lessen "suspicion, misinterpretation, and
animosity that, all too often in the past, characterized both
sides."[14]

Signs of openness for broader dialogue between liberal and
conservative Christians have emerged from various sources.
Douglas Jacobsen and William Vance Trollinger, Jr., of Messiah
College, call for "evangelicals to join with other Christian groups
in creating a middle ground, where all Christians can feel at home
and can be respected, without having to give up their distinctive
identities."[15] Joan Brown Campbell, general secretary of the National Council of Churches, advocates conversations among evangelical, pentecostal, and more mainline and orthodox Christians.
Her vision is not of a new bureaucratic organization, but sponta-
neous developments of Christians sitting around "a common table,
where we would sit together and find ways to work and speak
together."[16] Seeking a "middle ground," tempting as it sounds,
probably is too premature. Finding a "common table" would be a
major first step, so there can be genuine debate and disagreement
on issues of pivotal importance for the identity and life of the
church.

Conversion and Reconciliation

If a "middle ground" or a "common table" is to occur within
United Methodism, then both "liberals" and "evangelicals" need a
change of attitudes. Conversion and reconciliation are required on
both sides. If, for example, "liberals" interpret an openness for
dialogue among "evangelicals" as a "victory for their side, a sign
that evangelicals have finally seen the light, their attitude will not
only misrepresent what is happening with the evangelical world,
but may also undermine positive developments."[17] The same holds
true in reverse.

Many of us don't want to bridge the divide or heal the differences, either with persons outside our denomination or especially

with those within it. Our mistrust level overwhelms our capacity to trust. We ignore the Talmud's teaching that "charity equals all the other commandments." We want to forget Jesus' command to love one another as friends.

Building these bridges will not be easy, since relationships often are frozen between Christians of differing theologies within the denomination. But the task is imperative if we are to follow Jesus' command to love one another as friends. Sometimes it will require us to build hidden bridges, lest the participants drown due to the depth of suspicion and rancor.

I am uncertain whether we need a national denominational plan for conversation or dialogue between conservatives and liberals, but I am persuaded we need many individual, local, district, and conference initiatives which creatively consider the possibilities and enable persons and churches to move forward in bridge building between Christians wherever possible. This study book is designed as one resource in promoting this exchange of convictions and concerns.

During the last couple of years a small group of United Methodist laity and clergy, active in both local and general church matters, have met several times to explore what we could do to lessen the polarization and politicalization of our denomination. On matters of theology and social justice questions, we are often diametrically opposed. What united us is a love of Christ and the church. We have become increasingly concerned that our denomination has been on a path of self-destruction, with the gaps getting greater and greater. Too often General Conference has proved to be for all participants a painful and bitter experience of clashing perspectives and politics. Calling ourselves United Methodist Dialogue, this group of so-called evangelicals and liberals declared that

> what united us was a love for the Church and a concern about its increasingly destructive polarization. We decided to gather without an agenda except to pray together, list the issues that seem to divide us, and attempt to find ways to discuss them in a manner consistent with our calling as the Church and our tradition as United Methodists.[18]

I had long advocated such a gathering, but my commitment was immediately tested at the very first meeting when I discovered who the other people were in the room. I am ashamed to admit that I didn't really want to be reconciled with one of the participants. I still harbored anger in my heart from the last General Conference, when the two of us debated an issue for almost two weeks, and in a close vote he won. Why did he have to come? I favor dialogue with conservatives, but I didn't mean him! My spirit strayed far from the image of life together as friends cemented by Christ's love. But I had committed myself to this meeting, and I could hardly walk out without losing face, so I gritted my teeth and falsely smiled.

What happened that day far exceeded my expectations. We faced the toughest questions that plague the church—such as the church's teachings on homosexuality, biblical interpretation, Sophia and the Re-imagining Conference, and many other issues. We "achieved a degree of respect and understanding of one another's views we would not otherwise have had. We discovered that while our differences will continue, it is possible to discuss them in such a way that if consensus is where God is leading us, we will not be found resisting the Spirit."[19] We decided to meet again, and invited others to join us. We also agreed upon some strategies we thought might help the entire church diminish its tendencies toward polarization and politicalization.

But, what was truly significant for me was not so much the steps we were willing to take together publicly, but the conversion and reconciliation I felt in my heart. As the day progressed and we expressed our perspectives and passion on certain topics, we also began to express our personal and family concerns. We began to see each other not primarily as opponents in the church's political arena, but as fellow Christian sisters and brothers hurting and struggling with real-life issues. Beyond a doubt, the high spiritual moment came for me at the end of the day when I walked across the room and embraced the man I earlier had not even wanted at the table. It was a moment of conversion for me and reconciliation for us both. I continue to pray for God's blessings and grace on him and his family.

At the moment we hugged I discovered anew the meaning of Jesus when he taught us to "love one another" as friends. I hope for more such experiences of conversion and reconciliation, of becoming *amigos por Jesús*. I pray that every Christian in his or her own context and circumstance will seek to build bridges even under icy waters.

Essentials and Nonessentials

As a result of this "evangelical/liberal" dialogue, we recommended the 1996 General Conference explore and study the ecumenical watchword cited in the *Discipline* as parallel to John Wesley's teachings: "In essentials, unity; in non-essentials, liberty; and, in all things, charity."

Throughout church history when division and disunity have splintered the Body of Christ, prophets of toleration and unity have advocated this proverb. The Disciples of Christ denomination has emphasized this saying. During the Civil War, Abraham Lincoln cited it in his speeches and writings.[20] In chapter 1, Richard P. Heitzenrater has contributed an in-depth historical account of how this phrase has been associated with John Wesley and the Methodist movement over the years. Rosemary Keller addresses how Methodism has lost its essential oneness and needs to recover certain essential theological understandings.

Coined originally by Rupertus Meldenius during the Thirty Years' War that devastated the religious and political communities from 1618 to 1648, this epigram has been recited periodically over the years as a means of helping Christians define their core convictions and learn to live with their disagreements.[21]

Though "evangelicals" and "liberals" may accept this principle, past history demonstrates it will not prove simple to find agreement on the essentials and the nonessentials. However, it does provide a heuristic device or framework for conversation and dialogue. Hopefully, the spirit of charity or love can prevail even as we vigorously debate the critical questions of faith and life. As the journal of Henri Frederic Amiel reminds us: "Life is short and we have not much time for gladdening the hearts of those who travel the way with us. Oh, be swift to love! Make haste to be kind."[22]

The dilemma of defining essentials and nonessentials stems from the realization that not everyone agrees on what constitutes each category or by what criteria the differentiation should be made. Individual United Methodists do not concur in what are the absolute basics of the faith or even how much emphasis should be placed on accepted church documents or doctrines. Subscription to specific doctrines or creeds represents the utmost "essential" to Christian faith for many. Others would tread "lightly" in this area, believing the heart of Christian faith and life is discovered not in allegiance to ancient creeds but in active caring to the hungry, homeless, ill-clothed, and imprisoned, those Jesus designated as "the least of these" (Matt. 25:31-46). In chapter 2 both William Abraham and Mark Trotter emphasize doctrine as "essential," but they differ dramatically in their approaches, with Trotter accenting a minimum list and Abraham accentuating a maximum ledger.

Another type of essentials/nonessentials debate erupts periodically in the United States when for political reasons the government must partially close down because of unresolved budgetary disputes. "Essential" workers are mandated to stay at their jobs and "nonessential" employees are furloughed, under the assumption that some functions or duties of government are more imperative or important than others. Besides the disruptive costs in terms of service and morale, the issue of prioritizing becomes apparent. When New York City was on the edge of bankruptcy in 1975, it retained its police but laid off its bridge painters. This seemingly reasonable choice made sense until later bridges started to deteriorate and fall apart due to inadequate maintenance. Likewise, today many evangelical voices within United Methodism assert that lack of attention to "essential" doctrines since 1972 has corroded the denomination's unity, thus creating deterioration in its bridges of mission and ministry.

A second dilemma arises in defining the meaning of terms like *unity, liberty,* and *charity.* Again people approach each of these ideas from different presuppositions and perspectives. Abraham Lincoln illustrated this dilemma with a witty story about liberty:

> The shepherd drives the wolf from the sheep's throat, for which the sheep thanks the shepherd as his liberator, while the wolf denounces him for the same act. . . . Plainly the sheep and the wolf are not agreed upon a definition of liberty.[23]

Dialogue focused around the concepts of unity, liberty, and charity helps us discern different understandings and deepen our own perspectives. From quite different premises, Joy Moore and Harriett Olson in chapter 3 struggle with the meaning of "in non-essentials, liberty." How is individual conscience to be reconciled with church teachings? In chapter 4, Justo González and Maxie Dunnam agree that desiring "in all things, charity" does not mean unconditional acceptance of everything, though they demonstrate that charity or love can be interpreted quite differently.

Likewise, when it comes to envisioning what treasures should be preserved in United Methodism, Ruediger R. Minor and S. Michael Hahm in chapter 5 recite different dimensions of the tradition, though both underscore retaining an emphasis on mission. Divergence particularly becomes apparent in examining the essays in chapter 6 by Marjorie Hewitt Suchocki and Jerry Walls as they outline how United Methodists should change in the future. United Methodists along the "conservative/liberal" continuum agree neither on diagnosis nor on remedy for what ails the denomination.

Authors in this book present different facets of each of these concepts embedded in the phrase: "in essentials, unity; in non-essentials, liberty; and, in all things, charity." Readers, however, have certain advantages over the writers. You have an opportunity to review the historical background and varied usages of this phrase. Due to publishing time constraints, the authors did not. Likewise, you have another advantage in that you can weigh the competing arguments and perceptions of all the essayists, while those who contributed had no chance for such dialogue.

The structure of this study book is for authors of divergent theological convictions to address the same topic, followed by a short third section written by the editors, which rearticulates the main chapter themes and then offers a list of questions that possibly will stimulate individual thought and/or group discussion. Reading in reverse might even be helpful, looking at the editorial summary prior to exploring the position papers. We hope the book will encourage dialogue among fellow United Methodists, who today often are not even talking to one another, except in political or polemical ways.

Convictions and Conversations

Dialogue, however, proves more problematic than sometimes realized. Liberals and conservatives do not always understand the process in the same way. Liberals are generally advocates of dialogue:

> People from different backgrounds and perspectives agree to listen to each other, learn from each other, and keep the conversation going. There is no need for winners or losers. If conflict arises, the rules of conversation, not of doctrine, should ensure a faithful and fair outcome.[24]

Christians should "work through differences with open minds, assertiveness, and respect for each other."[25]

Conservative Christians, however, are uncomfortable with some of these assumptions. They believe certain Christian convictions are non-negotiable and dialogue can be dangerous. The problem they see in guidelines for discussions is that often

> they lack any concern for the preservation of truth. The guidelines render the subject of disagreement virtually irrelevant; they imply that the way in which we conduct ourselves as we share our disagreements is our primary concern.[26]

It is, of course, too simplistic to suggest that liberals are for conversation and conservatives opt for conviction. Obviously liberals have convictions and conservatives engage in conversations, but awareness of this conversation/conviction continuum makes us more realistic when we set forth necessary ground rules for dialogue.

Fortunately, United Methodists are not as suspicious about dialogue as are persons in some other denominations. Since the days of John Wesley, various types of dialogue have been encouraged. The church has taken seriously the scriptural command to "speak the truth in love," lest we be "tossed to and fro and blown about by every wind of doctrine, by people's trickery, by their craftiness in deceitful scheming" (Eph. 4:14). In recent years United Methodists have participated in international dialogues through the World Methodist Council with Roman Catholic, Lutheran, Reformed, Orthodox, and Anglican churches.[27] Missing has been the internal dialogue within the denomination between "evangelicals" and "liberals."

Intentional efforts must be initiated in the immediate future for United Methodists to dialogue together about what is essential and nonessential, learning to care for one another in love even when strongly disagreeing with each other. Rather than talking to one's sister or brother United Methodist, for some liberals it would be easier to talk to a neighboring Hindu or Muslim. For some evangelicals, the temptation is to talk only to other conservatives. But the time now has come for us to build bridges under our own icy waters.

Adapting insights from Kenneth Cracknell, my Iliff colleague Sally B. Geis and I have developed four principles of dialogue that enhance mutual understanding and can serve as the foundation for healthy rather than hurtful conversation.[28] *First, dialogue begins when people meet each other.* This principle reminds us that dialogue begins when people talk with each other. Although no individual represents "the" conservative or "the" liberal position, personal expressions of a faith stance are more useful to productive group decision making than abstract, theoretical religious conversations.

Second, dialogue depends upon mutual understanding and mutual trust. If one's goal is to overcome misunderstanding and develop or preserve friendships in the face of conflict then it is wise to choose gentle, healing words rather than sharp, hurtful ones during the discussion. Too often persons seem eager to find fault, to question the motives or integrity of others. Sometimes questions are raised not in order to learn but to embarrass, confuse, or harass others. Those who take pleasure in "winning" need to remember that creating losers in a Christian dialogue can only lead to greater conflict and more distrust.

Third, dialogue makes it possible to share in service to the community. Dialogue is not a secret weapon or a propaganda tool, but a way to remove barriers and reduce tension among persons so that divisions can be transcended and the church can be about its mission to the world.

Fourth, dialogue becomes the medium of authentic witness. Dialogue happens not just for its own sake but in order to promote honest understanding of differences. If we cannot be honest with each other, how can we truly love one another? John P. Burgess, writing in the *Christian Century* about the experience of Presbyterians attempting to bridge the chasm between conservatives and liberals, acknowledges that the tension between "conversation" and "conviction" can sometimes paralyze the denomination, but with some mutual forbearance it is possible to do some joint theological reflection and find common ground on some key issues. Burgess contends:

> Our work proceeds in the hope that people who find themselves in painful disagreement may nonetheless discover that they need each other's insights and abilities; that common commitments may prove to be stronger than particular differences; that those who differ may find that they need each other if they are to struggle honestly and openly with the complexities of the issues that divide them.[29]

Dialogue Integral and Imperative

Dialogue, which combines conversation and conviction, may be difficult and demanding, but it is integral to our Wesleyan tradition of a "catholic spirit" and imperative to our United Methodist future. In another context and time, John Wesley urged us to "reason together":

> And let us resolve in all our conversation, either with or concerning each other, to use only the language of love; to speak with all softness and tenderness, with the most endearing expression which is consistent with truth and sincerity.[30]

25

As Dietrich Bonhoeffer suggested in *Life Together*, the only way ahead is suffering with one another and bearing one another's pain.[31] To a divided church in Colossae, Paul wrote: "Bear with one another and. . . . Above all, clothe yourselves with love, which binds everything together in perfect harmony" (Col. 3:13-14).

Ultimately, however, the key to the future of United Methodism will not be what happens at any particular General Conference, but whether the Christian values of unity, liberty, and charity clearly manifest themselves within dedicated disciples of Jesus Christ, witnessing and working in the church and world.

NOTES

1. This introduction edits and expands on the author's article, "Building Bridges Under Icy Waters," in *Circuit Rider,* November 1995, pp. 4-5.

2. James Davison Hunter quoted in "Divided We Stand," *Chicago Tribune,* October 28, 1992, sec. 2, p. 2. See also James Davison Hunter, *Cultural Wars: The Struggle to Define America* (Basic Books, 1991), and Tom Sine, *Cease Fire: Searching for Sanity in America's Culture Wars* (Grand Rapids: Wm. B. Eerdmans Publishing Co., 1995).

3. This section repeats what I wrote with Sally B. Geis in a chapter entitled, "Can We Disagree in Love?" in a book we edited called *Caught in the Crossfire: Helping Christians Debate Homosexuality* (Nashville: Abingdon Press, 1994), pp. 14-15.

4. Robert Wuthnow, *The Restructuring of American Religion, Society and Faith Since World War II* (Princeton, N.J.: Princeton University Press, 1988), p. 132.

5. See Douglas Jacobsen, "What Culture War? The View from the Center," *Christian Century,* November 15, 1995, pp. 1082-85, for a critical analysis of the "cultural war" theory and an affirmation of the "vital center" within our churches.

6. Cited in *Context,* 18, 11 (June 1, 1986), p. 6.

7. Wuthnow, *Restructuring of American Religion,* p. 215.

8. Douglas Jacobsen and William Vance Trollinger, Jr., "Evangelical and Ecumenical: Re-forming a Center," *Christian Century,* July 13-20, 1994, p. 682.

9. Robert Wuthnow, *The Struggle for America's Soul* (Grand Rapids: Wm. B. Eerdmans Publishing Co., 1989), p. 185.

10. D. Moody Smith, "John," *Harper's Bible Commentary* (San Francisco: Harper & Row, 1988), p. 1069.

11. See Donald E. Messer, *A Conspiracy of Goodness: Contemporary Images of Christian Mission* (Nashville: Abingdon Press, 1992), pp. 91-108.

12. "Sosnovkin's Bridge," *Reader's Digest,* February, 1943, p. 86. Thanks to Wilson T. Boots for first telling me the story.

13. Marlin Van Elderen, "Building Bridges: The WCC and Evangelicals," *One World,* January-February, 1994, p. 8.

14. Kenneth S. Kantzer, "Should Roman Catholics and Evangelicals Join Ranks?" in *Christianity Today,* July 18, 1994, p. 17.

15. Jacobsen and Trollinger, "Evangelical and Ecumenical," p. 684.

16. "Ecumenical Climb: An Interview with Joan Brown Campbell," *Christian Century,* November 8, 1995, p. 1051.

17. Jacobsen and Trollinger, "Evangelical and Ecumenical," p. 684, are speaking about dialogue between evangelical and mainline churches, but their point applies equally well for internal denominational conversation.

18. Quotation from a joint letter dated November 14, 1994, and signed by the initial nine participants, inviting the others to join if they concurred.

19. Quotation from letter of November 14, 1994.

20. John Benjamin Rust, *The Great Peace Motto* (Cleveland: Central Publishing House, 1929), p. 9.

21. See Rust, *The Great Peace Motto,* pp. 55-56; and Winfred Ernest Garrison and Alfred T. DeGroot, *The Disciples of Christ: A History* (St. Louis: Bethany Press, 1948), pp. 40-41.

22. Quoted in *Context,* 20, 1 (January 1, 1988), p. 2.

23. Abraham Lincoln, address at the Sanitary Fair, Baltimore, April 18, 1864, reprinted in *The Wit and Wisdom of Abraham Lincoln,* ed. Alex Ayres (New York: Penguin Books, 1992), p. 119.

24. John P. Burgess, "Conversation, Conviction, and the Presbyterian Identity Crisis," *Christian Century,* February 24, 1993, p. 207.

25. Ibid.

26. Ibid.

27. See Geoffrey Wainwright, *Methodists in Dialog* (Nashville: Abingdon Press, 1995).

28. This next section on four principles of dialogue is cited verbatim with permission from Sally B. Geis and Donald E. Messer, eds., *Caught in the Crossfire: Helping Christians Debate Homosexuality* (Nashville: Abingdon Press, 1994), pp. 16-17. See Kenneth Cracknell, *Toward a New Relationship: Christians and People of Other Faith* (London: Epworth Press, 1986), pp. 110-27.

29. Burgess, "The Presbyterian Identity Crisis," p. 207.

30. "Letter to a Roman Catholic," *The Works of John Wesley,* ed. Thomas Jackson (Grand Rapids: Zondervan, 1958–59), 10:80-86, in particular 84-85.

31. Dietrich Bonhoeffer, *Life Together,* trans. John W. Doberstein (New York: Harper & Row, 1976), pp. 100-103.

1

"Unity, Liberty, Charity" in the Wesleyan Heritage
Richard P. Heitzenrater

"Can you tell me where Wesley said _____?" This request comes my way three to four times a month. As often as not, it seems, the saying in question turns out *not* to be an actual Wesley quotation, but one of many that are ascribed wrongly to him. That usually explains the difficulty the inquirer experienced trying to find the source in Wesley. So it was no surprise to have someone ask me where Wesley said or wrote the motto: "In essentials, unity; in non-essentials, liberty; and, in all things, charity." That question had come my way before, so I was fairly sure it was not in Wesley. But recently I have gained access to two or three new sources of detailed information (written indices and computer data banks) that together amount to a universal bibliographic search capability and a virtual concordance of Wesley's word usage. These sources confirmed my earlier impression that the saying was not used by Wesley. These tools also provided some direction for tracing the actual location of the motto.

No doubt the reason that the motto has lately been associated with Wesley is that it rings true to some recent Methodist/ecumenical understandings of Wesley's concept of "catholic spirit." The work of Colin Williams and Albert Outler, in particular, stressed the ecumenical implications of Wesley's perspective. It was quite natural, then, for the General Conference of 1972 to accept the proposed wording of "Our Theological Task" for Part II of the *Book of Discipline* as presented from a committee chaired by Outler— "United Methodists can heartily endorse the classical ecumenical watchword, 'In essentials, unity; in non-essentials, liberty; and, in all things, charity' (love that cares and understands)." That sentence has been subsequently read by some to mean that Wesley himself actually used those words at some place or time, which is neither implied in the sentence nor seems in fact to be the case. The ascription of the quotation to Wesley, however, is not the first wrong ascription to this motto. The history of the saying and its supposed source is an interesting story in itself.

The Origin of the Motto

One of the earliest sources to whom the "peace motto," as it is sometimes called, has been attributed is St. Augustine. However, just as Wesley was first connected with the quotation nearly two centuries after his own death, so also Augustine was apparently first associated with the saying a millennium or more after his death. Actually, there is some basis for connecting the quotation with Augustine. In his "Epistle to Januarius" he does differentiate between the truly catholic elements of the church's tradition, which are more binding since they were established by Christ, the apostles, and the Plenary Councils, and those less important elements that were dependent upon local church custom and were therefore exercised with more variety and freedom. Many people have tried to find the specific motto in Augustine, but without success.

The saying has also been ascribed to other well-known Christian writers, such as Vincent of Lerins and Philip Melanchthon, who exhibited irenic or ecumenical tendencies down through the centuries. But the actual motto has never been found in any writer of the early church, the medieval period, or even the first generation of Protestant reformers.

By the mid-nineteenth century, the attribution to Augustine was fairly conclusively disproved and the actual author was quite clearly designated.[1] By that time, several people had become fascinated by the quotation, not only for its applicability to their times and situations, but also out of interest in its elusive background and authorship. About 1850, Friedrich Luecke discovered that a Dutch scholar, W. Pieffer, had designated the actual source of the quotation as a work by Rupertus Meldenius. This obscure theologian of the sixteenth century had introduced the motto in

30

his treatise, *Paranaenesis votiva pro pace ecclesiae* ("Votive Precept for Church Peace"), written about 1627 in the midst of the Thirty Years' War.

The original treatise had, by the nineteenth century, been lost, but a reprint of it had been included in a collection of theological works published in Leipzig in the mid-eighteenth century. Luecke himself then republished the pamphlet in 1850 in *Ueber das Alter, den Verfasser, die urspruengliche Form und den wahren Sinn des kirchlichen Friedensspruches: In necessariis unitas, in non necessariis libertas, in utrisque caritas!* ("The Age, Author, Original Form, and True Meaning of the Churchly Peace Motto: . . ."). The following year, Luecke published a supplement *(Nachtrage uber den verfasser des spruches: In necessariis unitas, in non necessariis libertas, in utrisque caritas)* that looked further at the life and work of Meldenius, whose name had been recognized as a pseudonym by an eighteenth-century Swiss theologian, Samuel Werenfels. Meldenius' real name is now thought to be Petrus Meiderlinus.[2] In recent years, the saying has been readily cited to Meldenius or Meiderlinus.[3]

The Context of the Motto

The longtime mystery of the elusive author of the saying, however, was matched in the nineteenth and early twentieth century by a growing fascination with the meaning and applicability of the saying. Several persons recognized that the divisiveness and fragmentation of nineteenth-century religion matched the conditions to which Meldenius/Meiderlinus was speaking two centuries earlier. At that time, in the mid-1620s, the competition between religious confessions that were associated with established national churches had played a significant role in the outbreak of military hostilities in Europe. Meldenius hoped that nonpartisan (pious and moral) friends would answer the call to bolster the welfare of the Christian church, to advance the true purity of its doctrine, and to heal the wounds resulting from years of hostile conflict.[4]

Meldenius had a vision in which the devil tried to convince a Christian warrior that the elect must establish an order to protect the true apostolic faith confessionally, with strict observance of

31

doctrines and forms. Christ, however, then appeared to the warrior and told him simply to remain faithful to the pure Word of God, in simplicity and humility of heart.[5] Meldenius was concerned that zealous partisans to a particular confession often manifest a pretense of orthodoxy while acting in a manner that is destructive to Christianity. Those, however, who follow a simple counsel of moderation could build up the church through the Word of Truth by living a pure exemplary life in harmony with the true Christian faith. The former perspective results in "pharisaical hypocrisy" that leads to too much hunting of real or supposed heretics from the pulpit. The latter view, however, leads to humility and love, peace, and unity, and the recognition that the essential Christian doctrines (e.g., the articles of the Apostles' Creed) all point to love and lead to unity.[6]

Meldenius does not deny the necessity of combating errors and heresies in the church, but rather calls for "the genuine type of polemics, which is pious, prudent, moderate, careful and circumspect, and which does not disturb the edification of the congregations nor confuse the consciences." He feels that truth is won through the evidence of the spirit and of power, and not through quarrelsomeness. The church must indeed have doctrinal statements, especially pertaining to (1) articles of faith that are indispensable to salvation or (2) chief teachings of the catechism, insofar as these both are based on clear and unmistakable evidence from testimonies of Holy Scripture, sufficiently attended in the church, and lawfully formulated and promulgated by a free judicatory. The essentials are determined by a doctrinal consensus of the magisterium—everything is necessary upon which all truly believing theologians are agreed.[7]

The Meaning of the Motto

The motto directly addresses one of the knottiest problems in the relationship between various Christian perspectives, the matter of how Christians of different persuasions should relate to each other. At the heart of the issue is the question, What is essential to the Christian religion? Meldenius was trying to unite warring groups that had fragmented the Christian church into differentiated orthodoxies by urging them to focus on the essentials that they held in common. Both the focus and the dynamic of his concern, as we have seen, was love—*caritas*. But Luecke and Rust were both confronting the problem from a different angle, each living in a time when church unity was being proposed that would dissolve the distinctive denominational churches and merge them into an "undefined universal fellowship in which the most disparate thinking and teachings were to receive equal recognition." Rust saw this as creating an "empty coalition" in which the so-called (but misnamed) unity of discordant factions consisted in the right of each to think and let think.[8]

By thus ignoring the presence and authority of certain essential elements of Christianity, such a position ignores the first part of the motto. This approach empties unity of anything positively fundamental to the faith. And yet, to force adherence to basic principles without an allowance for freedom in nonessential matters would ignore the second part of the motto. That approach forces unity into a straitjacket of universalizing orthodoxy that is equally justifiable, but attempts to maintain the church by careful juridication and administration. Such an approach fails to take seriously the distinction between essentials and nonessentials at all. The absence of either part of the motto causes problems: there can be no true unity without an element of liberty on nonessentials; there can be no real liberty without the power of meaningful unity on essentials.[9] And both of these principles must be held together by the third principle, a universal attitude of charity.

The Motto Not Found in Wesley

Several people quoted the saying between 1526 and Wesley's day, including Gregorius Francus, J. A. Comenius, Richard Baxter, and Herman Witsius.[10] John Wesley, however, may never have read or heard this motto. The most likely source in which Wesley might have seen it was the writings of Richard Baxter, who had a lively zeal for peace and unity among Christians and whose writings Wesley read, recommended, and even published in abridged form.

Baxter used the motto in several publications, in both its Latin and English versions,[11] feeling that it represented "the true and only way of concord of all the Christian Churches." In the opening dedication to *The Saint's Everlasting Rest* (1649), the noncon-formist Baxter speaks of the discord between religious factions in England and provides ten directions that he feels would help bring peace. In suggestion five, he mentions the differences among four particular opinions as to the proper form of church government: moderate Presbyterian, Independent, Episcopal, and Erastian. He suggests that they try to come together as much as they can on their principles and to unite as far as may be in their practice. Where this is not possible, Baxter suggests that they agree on a "pacificatory enterprise," a loving, peaceable course by which to carry on their different practices. He then goes on to say: "so that (as Rup. Meldenius saith) we may have unity in things necessary, liberty in things unnecessary, and charity in all."[12] Although Wesley published an extract of this work, he included only the first two pages of Baxter's twelve-page dedication and totally omitted the ten "directions" and the reference to Meldenius' motto. In fact, when Wesley published another of Baxter's works, *A Call to the Unconverted,* he intentionally omitted a sentence in Baxter's pref-ace that one might have expected him to highlight: "If we be not all agreed about some ceremonies or forms of government, one would think that, before this, we should have been agreed to live a holy and heavenly life, in obedience to God, his work, and ministers, and in love and peace with one another."[13]

Besides omitting these quotations and sentiments from his abridged editions of Baxter's works, Wesley also seems never to have published the peace motto in any of his own writings. Nor did he ever appropriate Baxter's ideas on the matter of "essentials" found in Baxter's works, *Which Is the True Church* (1679, p. 14) and *Methodus Theologiae Christianae* (1681, pp. 12-16). However, Wesley would certainly have acknowledged the truth of Baxter's observation that "divines are divided [over] what are the points necessary to be believed explicitly" (*True Church,* p. 14).

One should not be surprised that Wesley does not cite the quotation on unity, liberty, and charity. He does not ever have very much good to say about "liberty," a concept that had been politi-cized in ways that he found distasteful. His often-quoted comment "We are no republicans" indicates a strong feeling that went deeper

34

than simply an aversion to the idea of the Methodist Conference voting on issues. Neither does Wesley have any particular fondness for the term "charity." In his sermon on the topic, he goes to some length explaining why the term is inappropriate as a substitute for "love."

But Wesley would have some sympathy for the general intent of the motto. He was concerned for the unity of the church; he did distinguish between essential and nonessential matters of religion; and he was constantly focused on the centrality of love.

Diversity in Early Methodism

From an early point in the Methodist revival, Wesley was confronted with the need to relate to various groups within Christianity. His movement was, of course, a part of the Church of England, of which he was a priest to the day he died. But persons from many other religious groups (Baptists, Quakers, Presbyterians, etc.) associated with the Methodists in the extraparochial activities within their societies. The only requirement of people joining the United Societies of the People Called Methodists was to demonstrate "a desire to flee from the wrath to come and be saved from your sins."

Wesley was increasingly proud of the openness of the requirements for joining with the Methodists. Toward the end of his life, he made frequent comments about the manner in which the Methodists "think and let think." Two points must be noted in this context, however: (1) Wesley is usually talking about *initiatory* requirements, drawing the contrast between the requirements for joining his movement (consisting of *societies*) and the requirements for joining various ecclesiastical organizations or *churches* that are typically defined by creed, articles, and confessions; and (2) he usually passes over the fact that *maintenance of good standing* in the societies, nevertheless, required that the members adhere to the General Rules and pass muster at quarterly examinations. And, of course, his comments on toleration are irrelevant to the matter of his expectations for his preachers, who were held to a tight line on matters of both doctrine and discipline.

35

Wesley's openness to religious association with others certainly had limits and was challenged by long-standing prejudices. He tried very hard to maintain uniformity in crucial matters of doctrine and discipline, among both his preachers and his people. There were Calvinist, Lutheran, Roman Catholic, and Moravian positions that he would not abide within Methodism. Annual conferences with his preachers resulted in published *Minutes* that spelled out the basic theological positions and organizational policies of the movement. Doctrinal standards set the boundaries of acceptable preaching among the people called Methodists. And his basic attitude toward the Roman Catholics demonstrated typical English xenophobia: politically, Roman Catholics were all potential traitors who could not be trusted.

But his own experiences with some Roman Catholics in Ireland in the middle of the eighteenth century changed his mind about the possibilities of relating to them as fellow Christians. His views on these matters appear most clearly in his "Letter to a Roman Catholic" and his sermon on "Catholic Spirit."

Wesley and the Catholic Spirit

One might have expected Wesley to find this motto appropriate for his movement, since (1) his societies were often themselves not unlike small ecumenical gatherings, and (2) his intent was to keep them within the parameters of the Church of England. Methodism in Great Britain in his day was not a church but a movement. It was much easier, then, for him to include persons of differing opinions on some matters. In fact, he was very proud of the fact that Methodism was open to a variety of opinions in some areas, while at the same time he held fast to the "grand doctrines" that he felt were essential. The distinction is most clearly delineated in his sermon on "Catholic Spirit."

Wesley wrote this sermon in the aftermath of a trip to Ireland, during which he had witnessed rioting in Cork. Although the riots stemmed from a mixture of political, economic, and religious issues, they were (as was and is often the case) typified as a clash between Catholics and Protestants. Dismayed by the blatant bigotry exhibited on both sides, Wesley tried to portray the Methodists as a persecuted though peace-loving people. The basis upon which he could extend the hand of fellowship to the Roman Catholics and others of different doctrinal persuasion from himself was his recognition that true religion was not to be located in any particular ecclesiastical combination of doctrine and polity. He could tolerate the "opinions" of others on subsidiary matters so long as they had a common sense of the "essentials" of the faith.

Wesley holds out no hope for an actual ecumenical union among different groups. He certainly recognized that "a difference in opinions or modes of worship may prevent an entire external union," yet he felt that a "union of affection" was possible. The key question is whether one's "heart is right" so that we can say, "Give me thine hand."[14] But even this first level of ecumenical affection had certain prerequisites. Wesley defines the question "Is thine heart right?" in terms of over sixty explicit questions that comprise seven full paragraphs of his sermon. A small sampling would include such questions as, Do you believe in the eternity, immensity, wisdom, power, justice, mercy, and truth of God? Do you know Jesus Christ and him crucified? Have you disclaimed your own righteousness? Do you love God? Do you seek all your happiness in him alone? Is God the center of your soul? The sum of all your desires? Has the love of God cast the love of the world out of your soul? Is your eye single in all things and always fixed on Jesus? Do you aim at the glory of God in all you do? Is your heart right toward your neighbor? Do you love your enemies and the enemies of God? Do you show your love by your works?[15] At the end of two pages of questions, Wesley concludes: "If thou art thus minded, may every Christian say . . . then 'thy heart is right, as my heart is with thy heart.' On this basis, he can then say, 'Give me thine hand.'"

We might notice that this first part of the sermon, laying out the basis for reaching out to Christians of other groups, speaks very little about beliefs or doctrines as such. Besides the questions, "Do you believe in . . . ," Wesley also asks more questions that start, "Do you know," "Do you love," "Do you aim," "Do you show." True religion, for Wesley, always goes beyond beliefs and entails "faith working through love." A shared experience of God's love provides the basis for ecumenical affection. Wesley had an ability to see all persons as children of God beyond the obvious labels that they wear.

The second part of the sermon then goes on to show that such affection between Christians does not require agreement on "opinions." Wesley does not expect, much less require, the Roman Catholic to agree with him on modes of worship and prayer, the Baptist to agree with him on the need for infant baptism, the Presbyterian to agree with him on the episcopal form of church government. Conformity with his views on these matters is not necessary in order to extend to them "the right hand of fellowship."[16] What becomes clear, by examining other places where Wesley reiterates this theme, is that he is trying to get Christians to focus on what he considers to be the central core of their religion—not their own particular creeds or "orthodoxies," not their own particular forms of the sacraments or liturgy, but rather on what distinguishes Christians "from the unbelieving world." As he says in the "Character of a Methodist" a decade before the sermon on catholic spirit, "from real Christians, of whatsoever denomination they be, we earnestly desire not to be distinguished at all." He pleads with Christians of all groups "that we be in no wise divided among ourselves. Is thy heart right, as my heart is with thine? I ask no farther question. If it be, give me thy hand. For opinions, or terms, let us not destroy the work of God. Dost thou love and serve God? It is enough. I give thee the right hand of fellowship."[17]

At the same time, Wesley distinguishes viable "opinions" from errors and heresies. Not all views are acceptable as tolerable "opinions." As he wrote in a letter to John Newton in May, 1765, "Whatever is 'compatible with love to Christ, and a work of grace,' I term an *opinion*." That sort of opinion would be distinguished from errors and heresies, which he would "take some pains to recover any one from." He was quick to point out in this *Farther Appeal, Part III* (1.9-11), that the Methodists, though not bigoted as to opinions, do hold right opinions. There is not to be found any heresies among them; not only are they free of Arianism and Socinianism, but of any heresies enumerated by Bishop Pearson's work on the Creed.

But even these distinctions concerning opinions and errors must be seen within two larger concerns for Wesley. First, as he goes on to tell Newton, "I would take much more pains to recover any one from sin. One who lives and dies in error, or in dissent from our Church, may yet be saved, but one who lives and dies in sin must perish." And second, the decision to dispute matters of opinion also depends on another important factor for Wesley, as he explained to James Clarke in July, 1756: "At present, I say, 'Keep your own opinion'; I mine. I do not desire you to dispute these points. Whether we shall dispute them hereafter, is another question: Perhaps we may, perhaps we may not. This will depend on a great variety of circumstances—particularly on a probability of success; for I am determined never to dispute at all, if I have no hope of convincing my opponent."[18]

And it becomes obvious that when Wesley talks about openness to various opinions, he is not really talking about tolerating diversity of opinion *within* particular churches or denominations. He in fact stresses that those of a truly catholic spirit are as "fixed as the sun as to [their] judgment concerning the main branches of Christian doctrine." They have "settled, consistent principles." They know "the first elements of the gospel of Christ." Persons of a truly catholic spirit hold firmly to modes of worship that they feel are the best (most scriptural and rational). They also exercise their own judgment in choosing to join a church that matches their principles. And they are as "fixed" in that congregation (with its forms, modes, and opinions) as they are in their principles.[19]

Essentials and Nonessentials in Wesley

Having seen that Wesley's main concern in distinguishing matters that are fundamentally "essential" from those that are simply "opinions" is to provide a basis for what he calls "catholic love" among Christians of all denominations, we might examine a bit closer just what he felt was essential. It is clear that in many instances his discussion of this topic boils down to a very simple answer: "Love of God and neighbor." However, he occasionally will be more particular and follow an approach similar to that of other theologians such as Melanchthon, who distinguished between essential teachings of the church (those scriptural truths that were the grounds of salvation), and nonessential teachings that belong to the realm of speculative theology and have no necessary connection with salvation.[20]

It would be difficult to give an accurate or comprehensive list of Wesley's "essentials," even those relating to "the scripture way of salvation," although his sermon of that title is probably the best concise summary of his theology in that regard. He also comes close to providing a summary of essential beliefs in his "Letter to a Roman Catholic," but that list seems simply to reiterate the articles of the Apostles' Creed. What he calls "the three grand doctrines" of Methodism—repentance, faith, and holiness (the porch of religion, the door of religion, and religion itself)— find a variety of other terminology in their different listings, including similar or related ideas such as original sin, the Atonement, justification by faith, the new birth, and sanctification. He sometimes uses very strong language to make his point, as in his *Treatise On Original Sin*: "Consequently, this Doctrine [of original sin] promotes (nay, and is absolutely, indispensably necessary to promote) the whole of that religion which the Son of God lived and died to establish."[21] Wesley also points out, in his sermon on the Trinity, "I do not see how it is possible for any to have vital religion who denies that these three are one."[22]

At other times, Wesley is content to use more general language to refer to those doctrines he considers essential to true or vital religion:

Go and learn *the first elements of the gospel of Christ* . . . (Catholic Spirit)

Keep to the *fundamental truths of Christianity,* insist upon the grand points . . . (letter to John Erskine, 1765)

Hold fast *the essentials of the faith once delivered to the saints* . . . (On the Death of Geo. Whitefield, III.1)

Let us insist upon *the fundamental doctrines of all boldness* . . . (Ibid., III.5)

Wesley's comments (the latter pointing to justification by faith and the new birth) refer to doctrines that were not matters of opinion but rather were articles of faith. These were the essential doctrines, the fundamental points. These represent more than an accidental survival—having endured the death of a thousand qualifications. These doctrines are the central affirmations of the apostolic witness.

But even these, as important and closely related to vital religion as they were, were not religion itself. Wesley was always careful, even in these matters, to keep a careful balance between essential beliefs and true religion, which he most often summarizes as scriptural holiness, love of God and neighbor, having the mind of Christ and walking as he walked. This last point in particular was the distinguishing mark that defined the true character of a Methodist.[23]

Applications of the Motto

In what ways might or might not this motto be applicable either to eighteenth-century British Methodism or to contemporary United Methodism? As we have seen, the "peace motto" (though not used by Wesley) has a certain kinship to Wesley's understanding of "catholic spirit," the attitude of religious affection that Wesley could exhibit toward persons of other religious persuasions. However, the context of Wesley's notion is quite different from that of Meldenius or most other persons who have used the motto. The more typical ecclesiastical context in which the "pacificatory" phrase is cited in order to promote toleration involves either (1) mediating persons caught in the competition between denominations or groups that are on otherwise equal ground and struggling with each other for authoritative position and power (these folks are often ignored by both those in power, even in their own group), or (2) persons from a small dissenting group who feel persecuted by a large established church (these nonconformist petitioners are often ignored by the entrenched power structure).

Wesley and his movement do not really fit into either of these categories, but rather present (as he was aware) a rather peculiar situation in which the British Methodist societies in his day were never a distinct church as such and therefore never had to deal with the organizational accoutrements of a separate ecclesiastical organization. At the same time, they were "connected" to Wesley and the established church and therefore never faced the legal or political problems of being dissenters. Wesley thus had more freedom to be tolerant and open-minded in attracting new members. However, he obviously was not so tolerant of those who did not live up to the required discipline of the movement—at his death, after more than fifty years of the revival, the Methodists counted only about 70,000 members on their roles, an increase of less than 1,200 per year out of a general population of over eight million.

But above all, one must recognize that the question of essentials and nonessentials can be asked in quite different ways and in very different contexts, with the appropriate expectation of very different answers. The question, (1) "What are the essentials that are necessary for salvation?" is not the same as, (2) "What are the essentials upon which an ecumenical relationship can be formed?" And the latter question is different from, (3) "What are the essentials that a denomination can expect its members to hold?" Although this latter question is not usually the context in which the peace motto has been applied, and questions of ecumenical union are not the same as questions of denominational unity, we have raised the question in this third manner since it is not being viewed in that context. Each of these three questions assumes a different understanding of, or level of, "essentials." As a result, the matter of "nonessentials" also takes on a different significance in each of these three areas. In each case, the definitions and lists to answer each of the three questions might be quite dissimilar, and the dividing line between categories for each of the three would probably be at notably different levels in each answer. The first question was Wesley's main concern throughout most of his life and thought, the second is the focus of his comments about "catholic spirit," and the third is hardly ever addressed by him, except perhaps in his providing Articles of Religion for Methodists in America.

Use of the Motto in the Wesleyan Tradition Today

The discussion at all three levels, however, could be useful to United Methodists if these distinctions are kept in mind. Unfortunately, the placement of the motto in Part II of the *Book of Discipline* shifted between its original insertion in 1972 to a new location and phrasing in 1988, which has served to confuse matters. In the first instance, the motto was used in paragraph 69, "Our Theological Task," as part of the description of United Methodism's ecumenical stance: "United Methodists can heartily endorse the classical ecumenical watchword, 'In essentials, unity; in non-essentials, liberty; and, in all things, charity' (love that cares and understands)." In 1988, the motto was shifted to the introductory section of paragraph 67, "Our Doctrinal History," claiming that, with regard to diversity of opinions, "Wesley followed a time-tested approach: 'In essentials, unity; in non-essentials, liberty; and in all things, charity.' " Besides correcting the punctuation and changing the introductory phrase, however, the placement of the motto in a new setting takes it out of its proper context of ecumenical discussions and places it in the misleading position of introducing a discussion of Wesleyan "Standards." The discussion in the *Discipline* also misses the crucial organizational and ecclesiastical distinction between Wesley's societies, which could have a very flexible approach to these matters, and the denominational or established churches of his day and ours, which have built-in ecclesiological presuppositions and expectations.

Although it may seem somewhat odd to find it necessary to use an ecumenical motto to promote peace within a denomination, perhaps the current effort will bear fruit. It should be recognized that, not unlike in Wesley's day, many United Methodists today were raised in other denominations, which may partially explain the presence of such a widespread diversity of opinions on many issues. But we are no longer an amalgam of extraparochial religious societies that are simply organized to spread scriptural holiness. We are a church and sometimes find it difficult to discover who we are as such. Whether we can ever be "fixed as the sun" in our understanding of our own opinions is a question that remains to be answered. But in the struggle for self-identity in a diversity of relationships, both within and without the church, the third part of the peace motto remains as important as ever: "In all things, love." As Wesley pointed out in his *Advice to an Englishman:*

> It is true, if [one's] conscience be misinformed, you should endeavour to inform him better. But whatever you do, let it be done in charity, in love and meekness of wisdom. Be zealous for God; but remember, that 'the wrath of man worketh not the righteousness of God'; that angry zeal, though opposing sin, is the servant of sin; that true zeal is only the flame of love. Let this be your truly Protestant zeal: While you abhor every kind and degree of persecution, let your heart burn with love to all mankind. (par. 14)

NOTES

1. John Benjamin Rust, *The Great Peace Motto: "In essentials, unity, in non-essentials, liberty, in both, charity"* (Cleveland: 1929), pp. 24, 40.

2. A. Eekhof, *De zinspreuk: In necessariis unitas, in non necessariis libertas, in utrisque caritas: eenheid "in het noodige, vrijheid in het niet noodige, in beide de liefde"; oorsprong, beteekenis en verbrieding* (Leiden: 1931), pp. 36-52.

3. See A. W. Powicke in Eekhof, *De zinspreuk,* p. 79; Douglas Horton, ed., *The Basic Formula for Church Union: In consensis unitas, in non consensis libertas, in utrisque caritas* (Chicago: 1938), p. 38; Winfred Ernest Garrison and Alfred T. DeGroot, *The Disciples of Christ: A History* (St. Louis: Bethany Press, 1948), p. 40.

4. Rust, *The Great Peace Motto,* p. 46.

5. Ibid., p. 45.

6. Ibid., p. 49.

7. Ibid., pp. 51-52.

8. Ibid., p. 62.

9. Ibid., pp. 61, 66.

10. Eekhof, *De Zinspreuk,* pp. 69-70.

11. Ibid.

12. Richard Baxter, *The Saints Everlasting Rest* (London: 1651), Dedication, par. 5.

13. Richard Baxter, *A Call to the Unconverted* (Hartford: 1851), p. 29.

14. John Wesley, *Sermons II,* in *The Bicentennial Edition of the Works of John Wesley,* Albert C. Outler, ed. (Nashville: Abingdon Press, 1984), 2:82.

15. Ibid., 2:87-89.

16. Ibid., 2:89-90.

17. John Wesley, *The Methodist Societies,* in *The Bicentennial Edition of the Works of John Wesley,* Rupert F. Davies, ed. (Nashville: Abingdon Press, 1989), 9:42.

18. John Wesley, *The Letters of the Rev. John Wesley,* John Telford, ed. (London: Epworth Press, 1931), 3:181-82.

19. Wesley, *Sermons,* 2:93-94.
20. Rust, *The Great Peace Motto,* p. 37.
21. John Wesley, *The Works of John Wesley,* Thomas Jackson, ed. (Grand Rapids: Zondervan, 1958), 9:312.
22. Wesley, *Sermons,* 2:386 (see also p. 376).
23. Wesley, *Societies,* pp. 35-37.

"Unity, Liberty, Charity" in the Wesleyan Heritage
Rosemary Skinner Keller

Whatever happened to the evangelical heritage rooted in John Wesley's mandate to Britain's first Methodist preachers in 1744?

> To reform the Nation, particularly the Church,
> and to spread scriptural holiness over the Land.[1]

And, today, how can United Methodism discover "in essentials, unity; in non-essentials, liberty; and, in all things, charity" without renewing its historical and theological evangelical emphasis?

The Situation in Our Churches Today

Evangelicalism, as it developed in the eighteenth century, was wholeheartedly concerned about personal spirituality and social responsibility. Both of these commitments have been at the heart of the United Methodist tradition from the origins of Wesley's movement in seventeenth-century England and throughout the eighteenth and nineteenth centuries in the United States. Increasingly in the twentieth century, however, the mainstream of United Methodism has given up the distinct and essential evangelical claim at the roots of our antecedent denominations. This applies to both "liberals" and "conservatives."

In mainstream United Methodist churches today, powerful words once applied to personal spiritual experience within our evangelical tradition—words such as *conversion, new birth, born again, sanctification,* and *perfection*—are never used. Today, most mainstream United Methodist preachers would be embarrassed to introduce these words in their sermons. Further, twentieth-

46

century words that are equivalents to traditional evangelical language have not been found to help people understand their faith experiences and spiritual journeys.

At the other extreme, there are mainstream United Methodists today who have strong Christian convictions that the churches need to advocate and work for social transformation. A few persons may belong to organizations that cross denominational lines, such as Sojourners and the Evangelical and Ecumenical Women's Caucus, that are considered on the left wing of the evangelical spectrum. But, no organizations exist within The United Methodist Church that identify evangelicalism with its historic social action roots.

The Challenge Confronting Mainstream United Methodism

In The United Methodist Church today we must face two realities regarding evangelicalism: (1) The essential unity of personal spirituality and social responsibility in our historic evangelical tradition has been lost. (2) Evangelicalism is identified with the right wing of the denomination and of Protestantism, where emphasis is placed almost entirely on personal conversion and doctrinal purity.

The recovery of the distinct evangelical heritage within the larger ecumenical church should be a major priority of The United Methodist Church at the end of the twentieth century. What would it mean to recover our evangelical heritage in the late 1990s?

The Meaning of Evangelical

To begin, we need to understand how the word *evangelical* has been used during three periods of its prominence in the history of Protestantism, and the way in which its meaning has been different during each period.[2] First, during the Reformation in the sixteenth century, evangelical was virtually synonymous with the emerging Protestant movement, particularly in its Lutheran wing, in reaction to what has now become the Roman Catholic Church. This identification prevails today in Germany and Latin America.

Second, during the eighteenth and nineteenth centuries, evangelicalism lay at the heart of the Great Awakenings and revival movements, particularly in Great Britain and North America. Wesleyanişm and the Methodist movement were prime manifestations. Evangelicalism was less a theological system than a way of life, appropriated through conversion, justifying grace, and the sanctified life.

A strong emphasis was placed by many upon social responsibility as well as personal spirituality, affirmed in Wesley's charge to "reform the Nation, particularly the Church; and to spread scriptural holiness over the Land." Jesus Christ was the incarnation of the good news and the bearer of the good news. His proclamation in beginning his ministry in Nazareth, as given in Luke 4, was the key scriptural foundation. It was applied both to persons' inward condition and to their outward physical circumstances:

> The Spirit of the Lord is upon me,
>   because he has anointed me
>   to bring good news to the poor.
> He has sent me to proclaim release to the captives
>   and recovery of sight to the blind,
>   to let the oppressed go free,
>   to proclaim the year of the Lord's favor. . . .
> Today this scripture has been fulfilled in your hearing.
>
> (vv. 18-19, 21)

The activist, socially reform-minded wing of Methodism in the United States became strong, both in politics and society as a whole, in the new republic. "The Age of Methodism" in the nineteenth century was often applied to the nation as a whole, as well as to the church.

A third meaning has become predominant in our day, identifying evangelicalism with a conservative theological wing within the churches and with politically and socially conservative views. The strong impact of an initially religious viewpoint is again significant. This contemporary understanding grew out of the fundamentalist/modernist controversy of the 1920s and 1930s, with the rise of Darwinism and biblical historical criticism supported by the liberal "modernist" wing of the churches.

The Calling of Jennie Fowler Willing

The unity of personal spirituality and social responsibility comes to life in persons' faith experiences and spiritual journeys. The story of one of our denominational ancestors, Jennie Fowler Willing, helps us learn from the past what this heritage could mean to persons convicted of an evangelical calling today. A laywoman of United Methodist ancestry, her eighty-two years from 1834 until 1916 spanned a large segment of the "Age of Methodism" in the nineteenth century and into the twentieth.

As a young woman, Jennie Fowler married a budding Methodist Episcopal pastor, William Willing. Together they spent the early years of his ministry in New York State and the mid and later years in Illinois. Seeing herself as timid and shy, she sought to fulfill her own ministry as a minister's wife through her husband's professional calling and career.

Then, Jennie Willing, nurtured in the church since childhood, had a conversion experience, leading her to respond to a full-fledged public calling and ministry of her own in church and social reform work. Conversion was equated in Jennie Fowler Willing's mind with a personal commitment to Christ coming in "the hour when I made that surrender."[3] In language typical of nineteenth century holiness persons, she related a quiet inner experience that occurred one afternoon when "the Holy Spirit sent His light into the depths of my soul," enabling her to be released from the goals of a woman's traditional middle-class lifestyle within the home to a broader field of God's usefulness in the world.

> There I was, planning to fit up my exquisite little room, in one corner, its walls padded to shut out the groans, and to shut in the delicacy and beauty that I hoped to gather about me. . . . I saw that selfishness like that could never get me into heaven. . . . When I saw that, I was enabled to say "I give it all up. Henceforth for me, only thy will, and thy work."

John Wesley and his seventeenth- and eighteenth-century followers would have called Willing's description of "a dainty little snuggery," in which she sought to bring around her a few choice friends, books, pictures, and pieces of music, as her condition in the natural state of humanity. And, in good evangelical Wesleyan language, Jennie was born again.

In her new birth, she pictured herself "in a hospital with scores of people who were dying, and there was no one to give them their medicine, or even a cup of cold water. I had been sent there under orders to help all whom I could possibly reach. . . . The pain of that surrender was so severe that a knife seemed to pierce my heart, and the tears leaped from my eyes," she wrote. "Let me add that all these years, just in proportion as I have held myself loyal to that surrender, has God given me richly to enjoy the things that I put aside to accept His will."

Jennie Fowler Willing's heart was "strangely warmed" that afternoon, in a way similar to John Wesley's experience at Aldersgate. Her conversion was not a dramatic, once-in-a-lifetime revelatory moment, so often mischaracterized as typically "evangelical." Rather, it was a quiet encounter with the Holy Spirit within her which gave her a new purpose to be continually nurtured throughout her life.

The essentials of an evangelical conversion experience were contained in Willing's personal testimony. She experienced herself convicted of the sin of selfishness and forgiven by God for her personal self-seeking. Further, she received the assurance of God's presence to bring her new life and to guide her into sanctification and perfection, not the promise of a sinless, perfected life, but of a growing motivation and maturity to fulfill God's greater purpose for her. In the process, Willing responded to God's gift of grace and committed herself to walk in the journey in faith.

Jennie Fowler Willing led a life of active, vigorous service to God and her neighbors. Her calling over several decades of her middle and older adult years was given, primarily, to founding, organizing, and coordinating the work of the newly formed Women's Foreign Missionary Society and Women's Home Missionary Society of the Methodist Episcopal Church. Through this commitment to the Methodist Episcopal Church, she sought to reform it from within by enabling it to be an institution of greater service to God and to all God's people.

Willing also taught English at Illinois Wesleyan University, worked in crusades of the Women's Christian Temperance Union, gained a local preacher's license, pastored a church in Chicago, and opened the New York Training School and Settlement House in Hell's Kitchen in New York City when she was sixty-one years old after her husband died. Her mission extended beyond the church to other agencies directed to serve the needs of persons of all classes.

Jennie Fowler Willing went further than most persons, either clergy or laity, in the church in her day and in the years to come in discerning the shortcomings of philanthropy and the relationship of middle-class reformers to oppressed and marginalized people in need. She anticipated those who would follow in her train even in the late twentieth century. "The subject race must be made to comprehend its own dignity," Willing wrote.

> The principle violated in human servitude is the inherent greatness of humanity, and they who are under can be trusted to rise to equality or superiority only as they apprehend this principle. . . . The liberator must also see so plainly the tremendous import of human life, that he will go down among the oppressed and share the obloquy of their wrongs, sustained by his belief in the intrinsic human royalty.[4]

In her prophetic evangelism, Willing challenged the church and its members, in the name of Christ, to overturn the evil institution of slavery in her day and to confront oppressive institutions of all kinds in generations to follow. Her primary commitment, as true of the most radical evangelical reformers of her day, lay in Galatians 3:28: "There is no longer Jew or Greek, there is no longer slave or free, there is no longer male and female; for all of you are one in Christ Jesus."

"To Reform the Nation, Particularly the Church"

Jennie Fowler Willing's commitment to the evangelical unity of personal spirituality and social responsibility enables us to return to John Wesley's mandate to his first Methodist preachers in Great Britain in 1744

> to reform the Nation, particularly the Church,
> and to spread scriptural holiness over the Land.

At the Christmas Conference of 1784, celebrating the founding of the Methodist Episcopal Church in America, the commission was changed to the one now better known:

> to reform the Continent, and to spread
> scriptural holiness over these Lands.

The Christmas Conference made two substitutions in Wesley's original commission: (1) "to reform the *Nation, particularly the Church*" was changed to *"Continent,"* and (2) to spread scriptural holiness over *"the Land"* was changed to *"these Lands."*

At first glance, the reformulation may seem inconsequential. But, was it? Which wording was more relevant to the United States in Jennie Fowler Willing's day and in our own?

The two mandates address two different realities of time and social location in the lives of Great Britain, the United States, and the churches. Wesley's words to the new preachers in America, delivered through the Methodist Episcopal Church's first bishops, Francis Asbury and Thomas Coke, were given almost immediately after the American Revolution, or War for Independence, and formation of the first government of "these United States."

The first American Methodists were oriented to the physical space of a continent.[5] They contemplated what it would mean to take the gospel message throughout a complex physical frontier of mountains, rivers, and forests sprinkled with frontier outposts and newly settled villages. They confronted many diverse and uncharted "lands." The United States as a political entity of a "nation" barely had been formed, and the preachers had not yet conceived that the church might need to challenge political, economic, and social structures in the name of Jesus Christ. More particularly, it had not dawned upon them that the church itself might become complacent and need to be reformed.

When John Wesley addressed the first Methodist preachers within the Church of England, his territory was the political entity of an established nation and an institutional church. Both had become too fat and self-satisfied to be concerned about oppressed persons in need: paupers, prisoners, men who had no jobs to support families, and women and children who had been abused and abandoned.

The nation needed to be reformed, but more particularly the Church of England needed to be revitalized. Evangelical agents of Christ had to be sent forth to convert, to bring new birth and transformed life, to an institution that had become conformed to the world. The historical reality confronting the Methodist preachers in Great Britain closely resembled that of the United States and its churches in the mid-nineteenth century of Willing's day and the late twentieth century of our times.

Call to Mission: Yesterday and Today

We turn to *The Book of Discipline of The United Methodist Church: 1992* for two further words that define John Wesley's ministry to help envision our mission as The United Methodist Church today. (1) Wesley was reticent to put too much emphasis upon rules and doctrine for Christians. "Discipline was not church law; it was a way of discipleship." (2) "For Wesley there is no religion but social religion; no holiness but social holiness."[6]

Methodism originated as an evangelical, revivalist movement, both in England and in America. It later became a church, not in order to affirm a particular confession of faith as have some denominations, but to more faithfully carry out its evangelistic mission.

Following in Wesley's train, we look to *The Book of Discipline* as "a way of discipleship" for envisioning today the essential unity of social religion and social holiness:

> Our struggles for human dignity and social reform have been a response to God's demand for love, mercy, and justice in the light of the Kingdom. We proclaim no *personal gospel* that fails to express itself in relevant social concerns; we proclaim no *social gospel* that does not include the personal transformation of sinners.[7]

The Mission Statement in our *Discipline* opens with the following paragraph, which could be described as a theology of mission, or a way of discipleship:

Mission is the action of God
  who creates out of love,
  who calls a covenant people community,
  who graciously redeems and reconciles a broken
    and sinful people in Jesus Christ, and who
    through the Holy Spirit calls the Church
    into being as the instrument of the good
    news of grace to all people.

Mission is also the church's grateful response
  to what God has done, is doing, and will do.

A grace-formed church is one which
    responsibly participates in God's action in
    and for the world.[8]

The *Discipline* acknowledges and celebrates the diversity of the people called United Methodists. But, in our diversity, there is essential unity: "We are held together by a shared inheritance and a common desire to participate in the creative and redemptive activity of God.

Our Task is to articulate our vision in a way that will draw us together as a people in mission."[9]

The most important historical lesson to apply to "Our Task" today grows out of the slavery crisis in the mid-nineteenth century. The churches from our Evangelical United Brethren background upheld the vision that "there is no longer slave or free . . . for all of you are one in Christ Jesus." Neither the Evangelical Association or the United Brethren would allow their members to own or trade slaves.

On the Methodist side, however, the slavery issue created a blight upon the church and its mission of social holiness. Afraid that the controversy would sunder the denomination, the bishops of the Methodist Episcopal Church declared in 1836 that they had "come to the solemn conviction that the only safe, scriptural, and prudent way for us, both as ministers and people, to take, is wholly to refrain from the agitating subject."[10]

Denial of the reality did not solve the problem. The denomination split in 1844 into the Methodist Episcopal Church and the

Methodist Episcopal Church South. It took almost one hundred years, until 1939, for the two branches to come together again into The Methodist Church. Then, the formation of the separate Central Jurisdiction for black churches again denied the essential oneness in Christ, even of all members of our denomination. This denial of our inherent unity was not overcome until the Central Jurisdiction was abolished in 1972 after the creation of The United Methodist Church.

Though United Methodism is institutionally one denomination today, we know that only in overcoming racism will the essential oneness in Jesus Christ be gained. The same parallels could be drawn in relationship to sexism, classism, and homophobia in the churches, as well as other issues that divide us in our evangelical mission of social holiness.

Finally, the *Discipline* never allows us to be theoretical and abstract in our historic commitment "to reform the Nation, particularly the Church; and to spread scriptural holiness over the Land." In defining "The Present Challenge to Theology in the Church," it states:

> In addition to historic tensions and conflicts that still require resolution, new issues continually arise that summon us to fresh theological inquiry. Daily we are presented with an array of concerns that challenge our proclamation of God's reign over all of human existence.[11]

What would it mean for us as United Methodists at the end of the twentieth century to take seriously John Wesley's mandate to Britain's first Methodist preachers in 1744

> to reform the Nation, particularly the Church, and to spread scriptural holiness over the Land?

NOTES

1. *Minutes of the [British] Methodist Conference, from the First, held in London, by the Late Rev. John Wesley, A.M., in the Year 1744,* 5 vols. (London: John Mason, 1862-64), 1:9.

2. Donald Dayton, "Whither Evangelicalism?" in *Sanctification and Liberation: Liberation Theologies in Light of the Wesleyan Tradition,* Theodore Runyon, ed. (Nashville: Abingdon, 1981), pp. 143-46.

3. Quoted in Joanne Brown, "Jennie Fowler Willing (1834–1916): Methodist Churchwoman and Reformer," a Ph.D. dissertation, Boston University, 1983.

4. Jennie Fowler Willing, *Diamond Dust* (Cincinnati: Walden & Stowe, 1880), p. 159.

5. See Russell E. Richey, *Early American Methodism* (Bloomington: Indiana University Press, 1991), chap. 3.

6. *The Book of Discipline of The United Methodist Church: 1992* (Nashville: The United Methodist Publishing House), pp. 47-48.

7. Ibid., p. 48.

8. Ibid., p. 85.

9. Ibid., p. 83.

10. See John G. McEllhenney, ed., *United Methodism in America: A Compact History* (Nashville: Abingdon, 1982), chap. 5.

11. *The Book of Discipline 1992,* p. 82.

STUDY GUIDE

In about 1627 Rupertus Meldenius penned the phrase "in essentials, unity; in non-essentials, liberty; and, in all things, charity." Though it parallels the "catholic spirit" of John Wesley, no evidence exists that Wesley ever quoted it. Sometimes called the "peace motto," Meldenius suggested it as a way of uniting fragmented and warring Christian groups.

John Wesley was proud that Methodism was open to a variety of opinions in some areas, but simultaneously held fast to the "grand doctrines" of the faith. Wesley did not define exactly what was "essential"; sometimes his prescription boiled down to "love of God and neighbor."

Richard P. Heitzenrater proposes three ways of asking the question of essentials and nonessentials. What are the essentials (1) that are necessary for salvation? (2) upon which an ecumenical relationship can be formed? and (3) that a denomination can expect its members to hold?

Rosemary Skinner Keller contends both "conservative" and "liberal" United Methodists have forsaken their historical and theological evangelical emphases. The denomination can discover its unity by renewing John Wesley's mission mandate of 1744: "To reform the Nation, particularly the Church, and to spread scriptural holiness over the Land."

Items for Reflection

1. What would it mean to have what John Wesley called a "catholic spirit," open to a variety of opinions, yet holding to the "grand doctrines" of the faith? *Learn to respect people where they are.*

2. In what ways do you agree or disagree that both "liberal" and "conservative" United Methodists have lost their historical and theological evangelical emphases? *We don't train church for Evangelism Pastors caught up in political arena*

3. In what ways may the "peace motto" be helpful or problematic in facing issues within the contemporary church? *We worry about what the congre will say*

4. Sketch and discuss three lists of possible answers to these questions: (a) What are the essentials that are necessary for salvation? (b) What are the essentials upon which an ecumenical relationship can be formed? (c) What are the essentials that a denomination can expect its members to hold? Note similarities and differences.

3.) I feel the peace motto will help us accept each others differences + look at one another as children of God.

4. salvation
faith / open to Holy Spirit
love for self, God + others
service to God

Ecumenical
love

denomination
love

repentance

2

Discerning Unity in
Essentials
William J. Abraham

I never cease to be amazed at how United Methodists manage to hang together. I have witnessed open division within Methodism in Ireland, when Independent Methodism emerged in the late sixties and early seventies in response to Irish Methodist participation in the ecumenical movement. Yet this example of division is the exception that proves the rule that Methodists are remarkably good at staying together. We have been champions of unity within and without our church.

This is indeed remarkable because on the surface, at least, United Methodists do not have many of those ecclesiastical features that are often identified as essential to unity. We do not have either a pope or a strong episcopal consciousness that forms the focus of unity. Nor do we have clarity currently about our doctrinal identity, or about the efficacy of the sacraments, or about missional priorities, which might galvanize us into one, united body. Rather, we have a whole network of forces pulling us in radically different directions. Thus we have a variety of well-organized caucuses and special interest groups, a host of theological and doctrinal proposals floating around with articulate advocates, and a number of potentially explosive issues that create enormous strain and tension. What is remarkable is the way we have been able to stay together all these years.

Bonds of Current Unity

Such unity cannot be accidental. As I speculate about the causes of unity, a long list of factors impresses me. I believe we can safely assert that the following are pertinent considerations:

58

1. There is an instinctive love among us for fellowship and harmony. United Methodists generally love to join together in small groups and to relate to one another as positively as possible. This creates familial bonds of affection, care, and love, which are crucial to the warmth of the tradition.

2. We delight in allowing as much freedom as possible to think and grow. Freedom of thought and action is, of course, a core value of North American culture, but it is also a long-standing commitment which was well summed up in Wesley's commitment to the catholic spirit and to his admonition to think and let think on issues that did not strike at the core of Christianity.

3. We nourish a deep aversion to conflict, to heresy hunting, and to exclusion. This in part stems from an antipathy to pain, but it also stems from the conviction that those who do not fit in should be given as much time and space as possible to discover the reality of God and the truth for themselves.

4. We have a very strong sense of connectionalism. This is an extraordinary force in the tradition. Both itinerancy and our extensive use of committee connect people across the church and the country, creating bonds of love and friendship which can last a lifetime.

5. We have harbored and cultivated an instinctive commitment to ecumenism as essential to witness in the contemporary world. United Methodists have been heavily involved in the ecumenical efforts of the last century; so much so that with a few exceptions they are totally committed to working for the visible, organic unity of the church.

6. We have been committed to a fragile ideology of pluralism or diversity. This has been virtually the core of our identity as a community. We have made a virtue out of our differences to the point where we have favored process over substance as the center of gravity of our tradition. Central to this operation has been a tacit acceptance of the Methodist quadrilateral as the heart of our theology. So long as we can appeal to scripture, tradition, experience, and reason, we have been thoroughly permissive with each other.

7. We possess a lasting pastoral capacity to turn a blind eye to the worst and always to hope for the best, all the while being ready

for every eventuality. In this we have tried to be as wise as serpents and innocent as doves, spending enormous efforts to keep the wheels of our organizations in good working order.

8. We utilize a continuous turnover of leadership at the local, annual conference, and general conference levels. This prevents factions emerging and fosters ownership of the internal life of the church across the generations.

9. We are committed legally to structural elements, especially property clauses and the pension fund, which were carefully designed to keep as much ownership as possible within the boundaries of the church as a whole. This is the bond of unity of last resort, preventing radicals and hotheaded leaders from explicit division should they be tempted in this direction.

Because these factors work together in the most subtle and unseen ways, it is precarious to make predictions about explicit divisions within United Methodism. Even though I think that there are very troubled waters ahead of us, we should pause before we believe the kind of talk that currently makes its way around the church. It is currently fashionable, for example, to draw quick comparisons between United Methodism and recent developments within the Southern Baptists. I find such comparisons facile and superficial, for they ignore crucial disanalogies between our ecclesial ethos and that of our friends in the Baptist tradition. To take the obvious difference, conservatives within United Methodism are different from their supposed counterparts among the Southern Baptists. Conservatives in United Methodism are much more like liberal evangelicals than they are like fundamentalists. This explains why they want to take the tradition and history of the church so seriously and why they oppose division and schism.

Having stressed how difficult it is for explicit division to happen within our ranks, it is salutary to remember that our unity is indeed a fragile unity. We have divided in the past, so any idea that we are somehow protected and secure is false. Moreover, it is clear that the current worries about division cannot be merely put down to apocalyptic sentiment, to scaremongering, or to sensationalist rhetoric. There are important developments in our culture, which taken together could well make inroads on those invisible threads that hold us together. Moreover, unity is not just the absence of conflict; it is a positive state for which we must work and strive. So, if we are to heed the scriptural admonition to maintain the unity of the faith in the bond of peace, we must not rest on our laurels but attend to this matter with prayerful care.

In doing so, we need to disabuse ourselves of the illusion that the property clauses and pension fund will be sufficient to hold us together forever. In one recent extraordinary case in Missouri, a local church found a way to use *The Book of Discipline*'s provision on the sale of local church property to prepare for leaving the Connection and taking the property with them. The aim was not to move out immediately, but to have this option in place for the local church should the General Conference take the kind of action the local church deemed intolerable. This move was clever in the extreme, even though the local bishop was equally clever in preempting the chosen option. Such a case shows that no juridical process is sufficiently perfect that it cannot be circumvented. In these circumstances it would be premature and naive to think that the courts of the land will settle the issue of pension rights in favor of one or another group in the church.

Creating Space for Essential Doctrines

United Methodists have remarkable agreement on the procedural arrangements, which are essential for any organization whether secular or religious. The essentials of the arrangements are laid out in *The Book of Discipline*. Our success in this arena stems from our common sense and our pragmatism. We are not committed to any normative account of how the church is to be organized. While we possess a form of episcopacy, this has never been considered constitutive of the church, a fact reflected in the absence of bishops from sister Methodist churches in England and Ireland. Besides, we have always found ways to adjust how episcopacy works from generation to generation. The powers of our bishops have been carefully circumscribed to stay in tune with the deep democratic sensibilities that govern our culture as a whole. Current debates about the place of the local church in relation to the conferences reflect a challenge to long-standing agreements about how the church as a whole acts as one body. It is too early to say what proposed changes might mean for our life together.

By far the most important issue related to our unity hinges on the convictions and doctrines which animate our internal structures and play themselves out in a host of decisions related to our life as a whole. For example, it is no accident that preaching is pivotal for those who are ordained—so much so that pastors are frequently referred to as preachers. This originally gained ground because our ancestors were convinced that Scripture was derived from divine revelation, that divine revelation was essential to true knowledge of God, that true knowledge of God was essential to conversion and salvation, and that conversion and salvation were intimately tied to the hearing of the good news of the gospel. The claim of Paul summed up much of what has been at stake for us. "But how are they to call on one in whom they have not believed? And how are they to believe in one of whom they have never heard? And how are they to hear without someone to proclaim him? And how are they to proclaim him unless they are sent?" (Rom. 10:14-15). So the emphasis on preaching has not been accidental; it has been informed and driven by deep theological convictions about revelation, scripture, the nature of salvation, the reality of divine action in the church here and now, and the like.

We must consider the importance of agreement in doctrine as essential to our life together. We are remarkably reluctant to face this crucial dimension of our corporate existence. While as a church we rightly invest enormous energy in scholarship, education, and teaching, we are extremely reluctant to acknowledge the necessary role of doctrine in the church as a whole. It is important to pause and explore this topic for a moment.

Some of our critics outside United Methodism tend to see this reluctance as an inevitable result of our history. They think that we were born in a revivalistic tradition that disparaged doctrine and truth and that was dominated by warm emotional experiences that were disconnected from the life of the mind. On this analysis the truly great theologians in the Protestant tradition were Luther and Calvin; Wesley was at best an evangelist, a revivalist, and a religious organizer of genius. Many United Methodists themselves have absorbed this myth, and they remain unconvinced by the recent attempt by Albert Outler and others to rescue Wesley from these charges and to restore him in all his complex colors as a genuine theologian.

There is no need to exaggerate the stature of Wesley as a theologian to overturn this kind of nonsense. All we need to do is to point out that the Evangelical Awakening which produced Methodism in the first place was deeply laced with a host of convictions and doctrines without which they would not have been able to identify the deep experiences of God of the kind to be found among our ancestors. It was, for example, precisely because they believed that they were made in the image of God and because they believed that their sins had been forgiven through Christ that early Methodists were so exuberant in their worship and fellowship. It was because they believed that God is at work to heal the nations that they refused to reduce their faith to private sphere and adopted causes of reform like the early opposition to slavery. It was because they were deeply convinced in the internal working of the Holy Spirit in their hearts that they clung so doggedly to assurance when they were despised as presumptuous nobodies who dared to claim their membership in the family of the living God. It was because they were committed to the real possibility of holiness and perfection in love in this life and not just the life to come that they struggled to articulate a remarkable doctrine of entire sanctification. Indeed, so committed have we been to certain moral truths that we have a high propensity to divide when others in the tradition do not go along with us. What this set of observations shows is that the whole Methodist movement is unintelligible when doctrinal convictions are set aside or ignored. Moreover, over the years we have produced a vast body of literature by theologians and teachers whose existence proves beyond a shadow of doubt that we have a rich heritage of doctrinal conviction and discussion.

Understanding the Opposition to Essential Doctrines

How then did it come about that we grew uneasy about being specific about doctrine as essential to our life together? How did we reach the point where it is a common claim among us that we are free to believe anything we like as United Methodists? How did it come about that so many believe that agreement in doctrine is not essential to unity?

The story behind this development is so very complex that I can only here touch the hem of its garment. At least five factors deserve mention. Let me mention them schematically. First, a general crisis of authority in our culture has led many members to reject the idea that the church as a whole can coerce opinion or belief. People must be free as human beings to believe as they like; doctrines cannot be imposed from on high; the individual conscience cannot be violated.

Second, the church must be a community of hospitality, welcoming all into its midst. Hence the idea of setting boundaries of belief is unacceptable. Barriers to communion and membership, if they must exist at all, should be kept to an absolute minimum.

Third, to insist on uniformity of doctrine and belief is to embrace fundamentalism. Whatever else United Methodism is, it must be a real alternative to the narrowness of fundamentalism. Fundamentalism is too anti-intellectual, too tied to conservative politics, and too restrictive to be acceptable. By contrast United Methodism must be committed to the life of the mind, open to new and creative ideas, and ready to adjust to the best insights that fresh inquiry in our culture delivers.

Fourth, adherence to a set of specific doctrines is a form of idolatry, for it suggests that the reality of God can be captured in propositions and language. God lies beyond all language. The mysterious reality of God cannot be expressed in a narrow set of doctrines laid out in some sort of theological system. Such systems are locating to the life of the mind, and they are idolatrous when taken as the ultimate truth about God.

Fifth, we are extremely reluctant to insist on any specific body of doctrine as essential to our identity because we have become divided on the credibility of our own early doctrinal convictions. Since the beginnings of Methodism a whole raft of extended criticisms has been directed at classical Christian teaching. In this arena it is convenient to divide the response to these criticisms into two camps, namely conservatives and liberals, the former clinging to the past and the latter changing to fit the demands of the present. Many folk never, of course, quite fit into these camps, but the convenience of this classification is obvious, for it high-lights in a simple and dramatic way the deep intellectual division in our ranks. In these circumstances the idea of there being an agreed body of doctrine is historically impossible. Some even want to argue that there was never at any time an agreed body of doctrine.

If we are ever to get clear on the proper place of doctrine as essential to the welfare of the church then it is imperative to meet this raft of objections head-on. Let me be brief and to the point.

The first objection is irrelevant. Contrary to much popular opinion, our beliefs are not directly under our control, so the idea of the church coercing us into believing is nonsense at the outset. Some people might coerce me into handing over my money, but they cannot coerce me into believing that two plus two equals five or that it is now raining in my backyard while I know fully well that it is not.

Second, the claim that the church as a community of hospitality cannot require doctrinal commitment is silly and unrealistic. We are right, for example, to insist that pastors believe in God, that they hold that all persons regardless of race are saved through Jesus Christ, that they be committed to the propositions that it is wrong to exploit sexually vulnerable teens. The church has always had moral and doctrinal standards one way or another.

Third, it is misleading to be carried away with the bogey of fundamentalism, as if the only two alternatives on offer are a narrow fundamentalism or an expansive vacuum between the ears. There are other highly credible alternatives to explore. In fact, the classical tradition of The United Methodist Church pro-vides a third way between a narrow fundamentalism and a vapid pluralism.

Fourth, to claim that it is impossible to capture the truth about God is a dangerous half-truth. No language can capture the full reality of God, but this does not mean that we know nothing about God, or that we cannot provide deep and accurate depictions of God in our doctrines. To insist that God is love is to describe God truly. God is not the moral equivalent of a sadist; God is perfect love. We really can know what God is like, and we are glad to tell the whole world about it as best we can, as the church has always done.

Finally, to say that there are various parties or groups within United Methodism who do not agree on this or that issue, says nothing about the doctrinal commitments of United Methodism. Only the General Conference speaks for the church as a whole, and it has spoken loudly and clearly about its doctrinal commitments. That we are unable to hear stems from a doctrinal amnesia from which we have suffered for several generations. Such amnesia has been one of two protective devices shielding us from the truth and providing a mask for those personal doctrinal crusades which we have wanted to impose on the church as a whole. The church has been and is in fact very clear about the essentials of doctrine; the sooner we face this the better.

The Quadrilateral as a Protective Device Displacing Essential Doctrine

The other protective device I have in mind is, of course, the effort to replace our actual doctrinal standards with the Methodist quadrilateral. In fact the very existence of the Quadrilateral and its place in our recent history shows how confused we are about essentials. On the one hand, we have pushed the line that we do not have any doctrines, and on the other, we have insisted that what makes one a true United Methodist is commitment to the Quadrilateral. The Quadrilateral, however, is itself a doctrine of a sort. To believe the Quadrilateral is to believe the assertion that all Christian doctrine is to be worked out by consulting Scripture, tradition, experience, and reason. To be sure, this is a doctrine about doctrine, but it is a doctrine nonetheless. It is really a complex teaching about the nature of religious knowledge or about how to resolve very tangled questions about religious authority.

The Quadrilateral has been, in fact, the basic working doctrine of United Methodism for the last generation. It is what many explicitly believe to be the doctrinal essentials of our tradition. On this score it is now an abject failure; although it will take time for this to sink in through the church as a whole. The Quadrilateral is a mistake in the field of religious knowledge, and it has no right even to be considered as a serious option in any debate about the essentials of United Methodism. This is a startling and radical proposal that will come as a shock to those who have been indoctrinated into the prevailing view of the matter. I can only here cut to the chase and give the briefest indication why this is the case.[1]

Questions about how we know what we know about God have long been discussed by Christians. Some appeal to religious experience, some to divine revelation, some to natural theology, some to a particular philosophical proposal, some to the infallibility of the church or the pope, and some to faith. To propose the Quadrilateral as the ground for Christian doctrine is to argue that somehow we have to appeal to Scripture, tradition, experience, and reason to justify our proposals. What is crucial to observe is that there has been and will be no agreement on how to resolve this general debate. We will argue about how we know what we know until kingdom come. Happily we have made great progress technically in this field within the philosophy of religion over the last years. In fact, I would argue as a philosopher that the progress has been quite revolutionary, paving the way for an intellectual recovery of nerve within the church, which has been long overdue.

In the light of these developments, the Quadrilateral is a superficial and unsophisticated proposal. It is a useful first effort, but it only begins to scratch the surface of what needs to be said. To take an obvious problem, the Quadrilateral says absolutely nothing about the place of divine revelation in religious knowledge. Yet, in my judgment at least, any attempt to leave out this dimension will leave us badly handicapped intellectually. However, the really crucial point to register is this: it is profoundly mistaken for the church to insist on one line in this debate. It is best left to competent discussion and debate within the wider boundaries of the church. Yet what we have done is try to impose a superficial theory of knowledge as our standard of doctrine.

Our Essential Doctrines

Even if the Quadrilateral really did do the job for us in the field of religious knowledge, this does not begin to establish it as essential doctrine. Only the church as a whole, speaking through the General Conference, can determine essential doctrine, just as only the church as a whole, speaking through the General Conference, can determine our position on political issues. The church carefully guarded against the adoption of a doctrine like the Quadrilateral by protecting its real doctrines when it developed restrictive rules about change. When we explore what doctrines we actually committed ourselves to as a body, then the issue is clear. We committed ourselves to *The Articles of Religion, The Confession of Faith,* and Wesley's *Standard Sermons* and *Explanatory Notes on the New Testament.* These are the essentials of doctrine to which we are committed constitutionally and historically. To ignore this is to be divorced from historical reality.

United Methodism need not be, then, a body wandering around still wondering what it accepts as essential doctrine. To summarize the actual content in a generous way, it is committed to the classical faith of the church developed in the patristic period, as represented, say, by the Trinity and the Incarnation. It is committed to the great verities of the gospel recovered at the Reformation, as represented, say, by prevenient grace and justification by faith. And it is committed to its own distinctive convictions derived from its own rich encounter with the gospel, as represented, say, by assurance and entire sanctification. On the question of religious knowledge, it takes a very modest stand, as is revealed in the relevant articles on Scripture. It professes to be a scriptural church, deriving its faith therefrom, and inviting the whole church to search the Scriptures for the truth it holds. It is this network of doctrines rather than the Quadrilateral that is the real antidote to fundamentalism on the one hand and to an overcommitment in the field of religious knowledge on the other.

There are, to be sure, other alternatives currently being proposed as our essential doctrines. Some have suggested that we are committed to the teaching of Wesley as the core of our doctrinal identity. Important as Wesley is, this is a bizarre suggestion. When our church was formed it had to decide what to do with Wesley's writings and teaching. Our forefathers and foremothers were very careful not to confine themselves to Wesley. In fact, the only material they took over was the *Sermons* and *Notes,* and, even then, these were carefully subordinated to the wider faith of the church as a form of secondary commentary. This is entirely in keeping with the spirit of Wesley, for he was utterly opposed to creating any kind of narrow sect built merely on his distinctive ideas or on his theology. To be committed merely or even primarily to the thought and teaching of John Wesley as our essentials would be intellectually and spiritually disastrous. We need the great universal, catholic faith of the church as our foundation.

Another suggestion is that the essentials of our tradition are captured in our commitment to conference. Committed to Christ, we then commit ourselves to each other in the covenant of conference and leave the rest to personal choice in history. Conference is indeed an essential in the arena of United Methodist polity, and conference should rightly be seen as having profound theological significance. Conference is more than a convenient way of making decisions; it is also a way of signifying our unity in Christ and our way of being in the world. However, it is bizarre to transform the conference into a theological doctrine or into the essentials of the faith. All our conferences already presuppose the commitment to the essentials laid out by the General Conference of the church at its inception. Moreover, no Christian community can survive for long on the kind of minimal and vague commitment to Christ suggested in this proposal. We need precisely the kind of rich and varied treasures already identified as essentials.

Exploiting the Full Value of Our Essentials

Given this suggestion, we need now to consider briefly some of the implications of our analysis. An obvious implication is that we must abandon our recent love affair with doctrinal pluralism. Getting over this love affair is a healthy development because, besides being incoherent, doctrinal pluralism has left us locked in endless conflict. We have been going round in circles, insecure in ourselves and distrustful of each other. Once we are clear on the core commitments of our church, then we can tackle afresh the work that we need to do together in evangelism, in social reform, and in other ministries. Moreover, we can relax about those personal and distinctive convictions and concerns which can be so important to us for a time. We can work on enriching our essentials by developing those particular insights that are the possession of various groups within the church as a whole.

With similar freedom we can tackle the host of questions introduced by new learning, fresh insights, new experiences, and novel problems. In the absence of agreed essentials, we tend to be tossed around, driven by this or that fad in the culture. Knowing that some matters are tethered in our tradition, we are set at liberty to explore the tradition itself, to evaluate its reception across the generations, and to explore how we are to relate it creatively to new situations. In recent years we have been rightly preoccupied by questions of race, gender, and sexual orientation. These issues will be with us for some time to come. But others will soon arise. We have not begun to address the intellectual questions suggested by the imperative to evangelize our post-Christian culture in the West. Nor have we come to terms with the new work in religious knowledge, which has left the Quadrilateral so outdated. Nor have we harvested the fresh truths brought to light by the charismatic movement. Being anchored in the essentials of doctrine and inheriting a long tradition of critical inquiry provide exactly the spur we need to avoid lapsing into a dead or fossilized orthodoxy.

Especially important in future developments is the need to look again at the whole question of canon and to explore afresh the place of canonical materials and practices both in early Christian history and in our own tradition. Part of the mistake of the recent past was to be obsessed with questions of knowledge and justification. This has warped our reception of Scripture, and it has cut Scripture loose from its delicate relations with worship, prayer, sacramental life, and the struggle for holiness. I find it fascinating that our General Rules, another essential component of our tradition constitutionally, is a marvelous summary of the advice that crops up in the spiritual direction of the great saints of the church. I do not think it an accident that early Methodists who took this seriously often awakened to a deep encounter with God for themselves. The Rules provide the Holy Spirit a means for cleansing and restoring the eyes of faith. Hence it is natural that those who follow them will come to see God. What is at stake here is the simple but revolutionary idea that the Scriptures must be received as part of the rich tapestry of tradition, and that the whole tradition needs to be received primarily as a means of grace designed by God to make us wise unto salvation and equip us for every good work. Only as we grasp this in all its complexity can we turn to the normative place of Scripture as a medium of divine revelation and explore how revelation is related to reason, the testimony of tradition, and experience.

Another way to state the main point at issue here is to note that our Scriptures, our doctrine, our spiritual disciplines, our sacraments, and the like, are like a medicine to cure us of our bondage and restore in us the image and likeness of God. These are not primarily items to be worked in and out of debates in the theory of religious knowledge. They are delicate gifts of the Holy Spirit to be received in faith, to be pondered in our hearts, and to be worked into our pilgrim way in love for God and neighbor. That is why our doctrines can be accepted without being believed. This will be as tough a lesson for the zealous conservative keen to defend her orthodoxy as it will be for the independent liberal who is quick to profess his incredulity and unbelief. The deep intellectual treasures of the faith are not picked up casually on the run; nor is it wise to dismiss them at the first sign of intellectual trouble. We grow into them as much as we accept them and try them on for ourselves in our encounter with God. This is one more reason why it was so natural that the General Conference identified so carefully the normative doctrines of the tradition and took great care that they not be dislodged at will thereafter.

This outline of the delicate place of essential doctrine in the economy of the church does nothing of course to respond to those persons who have come to believe that our essential doctrines are outdated, false, or oppressive. There is, of course, room for fresh interpretation, for the filling out of additional insight garnered over the years, and for the tackling of all sorts of new questions and queries. Such developments explain in part why our tradition has assiduously cultivated the life of the mind through universities and publishing. However, there may come a point when our essential doctrines come to be seen as incredible or when they come to be held as so infected, say, with patriarchy that they are thought to be poisonous and dangerous. So what do we do if many have

71

ceased to believe the essentials, or if they have become an embar-
rassment to us? What do we do when even the best trained
theologians cannot reinterpret them to suit their own purposes,
or when the leadership of the church quietly relegates them to the
storage room of history? When this begins to happen on a significant scale then it is clear that the tradition as a whole is in serious
trouble. Our current turmoil suggests that this may well be the
case with the essentials of United Methodist doctrine. We can
envisage one of two things happening in the wake of this. Either
the tradition will slowly disintegrate from within, doing its best
initially to cover up reality by talk of pluralism or by disclaiming
commitment to essential doctrine. All that will be needed to
expose the disintegration is a trip wire to set off the explosion,
which will lead to the breakup of the tradition. Alternatively, the
tradition will find a way to encounter afresh its essential doctrines
and imaginatively own them for use in a new day. Only God knows
which of these options is in store for us in United Methodism in
the years ahead. Renewal and hope clearly lie ahead of us if we
can find a way in love to embrace this second, exciting option.

NOTE

1. I have discussed the value of the Quadrilateral at greater length in my
*Waking from Doctrinal Amnesia: The Healing of Doctrine in The United Methodist
Church* (Nashville: Abingdon Press, 1995).

Discerning Unity in Essentials
Mark Trotter

The situation in the church today is sometimes described as the loss of identity. Perhaps a better diagnosis is that in the face of the great social upheavals in the world during the last half century, the church has been unable to articulate a saving word. In contrast, Wesley and all the other reformers in their time were able to understand the world sufficiently to speak clearly a message that changed the world.

It is also significant to note that every reformer, including Wesley, lived in a time of historical crisis, the end of one era and the beginning of another. Augustine lived at the end of the Roman Empire and the beginning of the Middle Ages. Luther lived at the end of the Middle Ages and the rise of nation states. And Wesley lived at the beginning of the Enlightenment and the Industrial Revolution in England. In each case, the church recovered its identity through the theological struggle to shape the Christian message to be heard in a new world.

Reformation doesn't happen simply by adopting what previous generations have considered essential. Reformation comes when, in returning to the sources, we discover what is essential in proclaiming the gospel to the present age.

Wesley preached to an England being transformed by the Enlightenment and the Industrial Revolution. He directed his message to the realities of that world. In the same century, an American, Francis Asbury, preached to a culture that thought of itself as European and homogeneous, in spite of the presence of Africans, Native Americans, and Hispanics. We face a world that has been termed post-Enlightenment, postindustrial, and an

America that can no longer pretend to be homogeneous in population or culture, but is becoming perhaps the most pluralistic society in the world.

The church will recover its identity when we find the voice that will speak simply and clearly the meaning of the gospel to the world emerging in our time. Wesley was single-minded in preaching the gospel to his society. That is why he had no patience with theological disputes. They distracted from the main business. He made the distinction between "historical doctrines" and "saving faith." Essentials for him were those doctrines that interpreted for his world a saving faith. On everything else, Christians, he said, could "think and let think."

Three Essentials Necessary for This Age

In that spirit I will suggest three essentials necessary to preach the gospel to this age. Albert Outler, in *Theology in the Wesleyan Spirit*, suggests that Wesley also had only three.[1] Other scholars compile longer lists. Some include the core doctrines of orthodox Christianity, such as the centrality of Christ and the authority of Scripture. If one were to define "essential" in the Wesleyan sense of articulating "saving faith," then these doctrines are more appropriately classified as "foundational doctrines." They are, in a sense, "given," in that there is universal agreement among Christians on their importance, and assent to them is required for membership in the church. One might argue as to which doctrines would be classified as foundational doctrines, but that is not the task of a discussion on essentials. Foundational doctrines are catechesis, not proclamation. Essentials are tied to proclaiming the gospel to the world.

Other lists include Wesleyan emphases, such as "assurance" and "prevenient grace." They are doctrines that are derivative of the essentials, in that they answer questions posed by the essentials. Wesley dwelt on them because they had particular significance for his context, but they do not necessarily have the same importance in other situations, e.g., in a time no longer dominated by a rigid Calvinistic understanding of grace.

Justification

The first essential in every context is *justification by faith in God's grace alone*. It is significant to note that this doctrine was rediscovered at every moment of reformation in church history, including the Methodist revolution in the eighteenth century. At Aldersgate, John Wesley was converted by its message of liberating grace.

Surprisingly, Wesley was raised in a tradition relatively ignorant of "justification," and unimpressed with it. Outler describes Wesley's understanding of the process of salvation prior to Aldersgate as the "gospel of moral rectitude," which implied that one had the possibility of choosing the good and doing it. In that framework, the purpose of the church was to define the good through its preaching and teaching, and then provide help in achieving it through the grace available in the sacraments.

If that is an accurate description of the Anglicanism in which Wesley was raised and ordained a priest, it is apparent that in an Orwellian reversal, the Methodists in America have become the Anglicans they sought to reform two hundred years ago. It has been my observation that justification by grace is hardly understood, much less experienced by United Methodists in its radical, life-transforming power.

This classical interpretation of what God has done for us in Jesus Christ has been the touchstone of every renewal of the church. If we are to be renewed, we must not only agree on the centrality of justification by faith in God's grace, but also seek to experience its power in our own lives with the same single-mindedness that characterized Wesley's search.

Original Sin

The *doctrine of original sin* is a second essential, and the concomitant doctrine to justification in orthodox Protestant Christianity. Wesley considered it essential for understanding why we need salvation. Aldersgate not only warmed his heart, it also opened his eyes to the insidiousness and pervasiveness of sin. If one must depend totally on God's grace for salvation, then one is incapable of gaining it by oneself. The effort to do so resulted in despair in all the reformers, including Wesley.

Original sin is one of the essentials because it is necessary for understanding both the world to which we take the gospel, and those who take it there. We have the benefit of the writings of theologians, such as Reinhold Niebuhr and the Christian Realists, who have interpreted the doctrine in light of the history of the twentieth century. Their analysis should enable us to look realistically at the structures of society so as to see the subtle manifestation of sin in all institutions, including the most revered and venerated.

At present, United Methodists are divided in the way we preach redemption. Some put a strong emphasis on individual salvation, even to the point of believing that all that is necessary is to convert individuals one by one, and the problems of the world will be solved. Others are cynical about personal salvation and say the redemption of the world will come through bringing justice to the structures of society. The doctrine of original sin, interpreted in light of contemporary experience, will enable us to see that both are half-truths. Sin permeates all of life sufficiently to be declared "systemic," which means well-meaning individuals, even converted ones, will not be able to rid institutions of evil by the sincerity of their witness. But, on the other hand, bringing justice to institutions will not heal the personal contradictions in the human soul caused by our alienation from God.

Taking original sin seriously will not only strengthen our mission to the world, it will also aid our efforts in overcoming the divisions among us. An orthodox understanding of sin points to the corruption of even the best intentions of the religious. While Wesley used his understanding of original sin primarily to argue the universal need of salvation, he was not naive about its persistence after conversion.

Wesley's sermon "Catholic Spirit" is an exposition of 2 Kings 10:15. He sticks to the structure of the text to say that what is in one's heart is more important than "opinions," the doctrinal, ecclesiastical, and liturgical issues that divide Christians. But in the first section of the sermon he does mention that the human condition precludes certainty in religious matters. He makes reference to "invincible prejudice," a manifestation of sin, and to Paul's caution in 1 Corinthians that as human beings we see only "in part."

Whereas Wesley did not explore the relevance of original sin and human finiteness as they relate to knowledge and certainty, the cataclysmic events of the twentieth century have led theologians in our time to do so. We also have the benefit of the work of psychology and philosophy not available to Wesley and cautioning a similar realism about the limitations of human knowledge. The salutary benefit of this analysis is a healthy skepticism about certainty in matters theological, which should lead to a humility about one's own theological conclusions and a graciousness toward those who differ.

Sanctification of All of Life

The third essential is the *sanctification of all of life*. Wesley identified justification as the work God does *for* us, and sanctification as the work God does *in* us. Sanctification, often scorned by theologians in the Reformation tradition, is, in fact, an important corrective to the excessive reliance on grace, which, in Wesley's day, resulted in antinomianism and quietism. In our day it has a secular manifestation in what has been called the "triumph of the therapeutic." The therapeutic culture is based on the psychoanalytic technique of nonjudgmental acceptance. Paul Tillich used the language of psychology to translate justification by faith in God's grace into a contemporary idiom. He said it meant "accept the fact that you are accepted, even though you feel unacceptable." It is a powerful affirmation, and not a bad interpretation of justification. The problem with it, and the problem with a therapeutic culture, is that "acceptance" becomes an end in itself, the same situation Wesley encountered among the Reformation theologies that emphasized *sola gratia* to the point that any effort to improve one's life was theologically suspect as "works righteousness."

Sanctification was designed to correct that abuse by affirming that God's grace continues to work in our lives after conversion to bring us to perfection in love, defined in terms of the Great Commandment, loving God and our neighbor.

Wesley also insisted that sanctification had to do with all of life. Methodists sometimes divide on this, some seeing sanctification in terms of personal holiness, and others in terms of social holiness. Wesley would not let the two be separated. If we would be Christian we must take Christian transformation seriously, both in our personal life, and in the world in which we live. It may still take different forms. Some will not stray from Wesley's models of sanctification. Others will insist we live in a world that requires new ways to manifest love of God and neighbor.

Promoting Unity by Agreeing to These Essentials

What would promote unity among us would be an agreement that salvation by grace, followed by sanctification of personal and social life, are essential to the mission of the church to this age. These two, joined with a realistic understanding of sin that recognizes its power to sublimate "invincible ignorance" and interpose pride into discussions of matters theological, should enable us to give our attention to the central task of "reforming the continent, and spreading scriptural holiness across the land."

NOTE

1. Albert C. Outler, *Theology in the Wesleyan Spirit* (Nashville: Tidings, 1975), p. 23.

STUDY GUIDE

Theological doctrines—not organization or agreement on social issues—are identified as essentials for unity within United Methodism. Evangelicals call for a recovery of and fresh encounter with the great truths of the faith neglected or forgotten in the present. Liberals believe that simply repeating past creeds is insufficient, but that basic doctrines must be rearticulated in meaningful ways to communicate to the present generations.

Abraham explores current bonds of unity within the church, but criticizes the failure to make doctrine essential. He asserts that the

Methodist quadrilateral (Scripture primary, tradition, experience, and reason) has replaced actual doctrinal standards within United Methodism. He emphasizes the essentials to be *The Articles of Religion, The Confession of Faith,* and John Wesley's *Standard Sermons* and *Explanatory Notes on the New Testament.*

Trotter believes the essentials of the faith emerge in the context of preaching to the present age, not by simply adopting what previous generations have deemed essential. John Wesley distinguished between "historical doctrines" and "saving faith." Instead of a long list, Trotter cites three essential convictions that promote unity: justification by faith in God's grace alone, the doctrine of original sin, and the sanctification of all of life.

Items for Reflection

1. Do you feel basic doctrines of the Christian faith are being ignored or distorted in contemporary United Methodism?

2. What do you believe to be essential to future unity within the church? Are doctrines essential?

3. What does it mean to say that "doctrines can be accepted without being believed"?

4. In your judgment, has the Quadrilateral method become a doctrine itself?

5. What does it mean to assert that United Methodists in the United States "have become the Anglicans they sought to reform two hundred years ago"?

3

Discovering Liberty in Nonessentials
Harriett J. Olson

The problems of reconciling individual liberty of conscience with keeping faith with a community and its traditions must be endemic to religious life and practice. We have only to look to the New Testament to find examples of differences in practice and understanding that caused friction.

Jesus was criticized for not requiring strict fasting of his disciples while the disciples of John observed many dietary restrictions. The story of an encounter between Jesus and the disciples of John is recorded in three of the four Gospels (Matt. 9:14-17; Mark 2:18-22; Luke 5:33-39). The texts do not indicate that Jesus was criticizing the behavior of the disciples of John, but that he was explaining why it was appropriate for his own followers not to fast. Paul deals with a similar issue related to meat offered to idols (1 Cor. 8). Paul reasons that because all food is a gift of God it may properly be received by the believer with gratitude; however, for the sake of the weaker believers, all members of the body are urged to attend to the conscience of the person who raises the concern.

On a Faith Journey

How are we to live out and live into our faith as a body of believers within The United Methodist Church today? Each of us is on a faith journey that is both individual and corporate. We are members of the Body of Christ, each with gifts and callings, while we are all together named by the One Name. Herein lies a difficulty. Each of us individually is called to be engaged in a transforming relationship with God, through Jesus Christ, that has radical implications for our life and thought. We are each working out our own salvation (see Phil. 2:12). In order for us to proceed in this way, we each must make decisions about issues and actions that reflect and affect our walk with God. At the same time we are part of a community of believers, the church, with whom God is engaged. To some degree, God deals with us as a community. We receive a variety of spiritual gifts, and this "manifestation of the Spirit [is] for the common good" (1 Cor. 12:7). We are meant to be part of the body of believers, and our beliefs and our actions must affect and be affected by the beliefs of the whole church.

Going Beyond Blind Men Describing an Elephant

Of course, we could choose not to be affected by the broader church. Idiosyncratic expressions of faith abound. In congregational systems, individual churches develop their own faith expressions and they may choose to associate with other congregations or not. However, this approach presents the risk that is illustrated by the story of the blind men who encounter an elephant. As they touch the elephant one concludes that it is tall and round like a tree, another that it is broad and flat like a wall, the third that it is slender and wiggly like a snake. Encountering first the elephant's leg, side, or trunk, each generalizes his observation, and soon each concludes that the others are in error, or that there is more than one animal on the road. To base conclusions about how Christians should act in the world or about what Scripture might teach us today on the views of a small group of like-minded individuals is to risk describing the elephant as a slender, wiggly creature like a snake. While all believers have a common knowledge base about God from the Scriptures, our experiences and our understandings of Scripture may be as different as the elephant's trunk, leg, and side. We need broad dialogue to get as complete an understanding as possible. This leaves us with the same question that Paul was addressing: how are we to receive and act on the liberty that we have as individuals, and yet continue to be formed by the tradition and experience of the community?

Liberty and Freedom Critical for Theological Growth

Reflecting on this topic brought to mind an evening when I was still in high school. I sat with the parents of one of my friends, both of whom were pastors serving congregations at the time, and argued that the parables were "true." To me this meant that they were stories of events that had actually occurred. I felt that this proposition was pivotal to my understandings of scriptural authority and Jesus' own integrity. We discussed this topic with some fervor (I can only hope that I was polite as well as ardent), and none of us was persuaded by the others. We agreed to disagree. I do not have any clear recollection of what was said that evening; however, I left their home with the knowledge that these adults, these ordained people, these parents of my friend were willing to listen to me and to think about what I thought and to deal with my positions directly.

Since that time I have learned a little about rabbinical teaching methods and about different ways to communicate "truth." My friend's parents are now my friends too, and we still discuss difficult questions of faith. We still probably have different views of the authority of Scripture and a variety of other things, but we have long since become comfortable with leaving some matters unresolved. I am certain, however, that we would not be having these conversations if they had patronized me or had tried to make their understanding part of a required orthodoxy for me. Instead, they concluded that God was working in my life. They trusted that God would continue to call me, that God and the church would provide me with good teaching, and that they did not have to "fix" my beliefs.

I am not really suggesting that this one experience is a model for all of church life, nor am I suggesting that we can amble amiably along together waiting for persons with whom we may disagree to "grow up" in their faith. What I am suggesting is that how we conduct these discussions, and the degree of freedom or "liberty" that persons are accorded as they explore theological issues, will have a great impact on their own growth and maturity and on the growth in grace of the church. In the discussions about fasting and eating meat offered to idols mentioned above, neither Jesus nor

82

Paul insisted that the same practices be observed by all the believers. Jesus seems to have been content for two sets of appropriate observances to proceed side by side, while Paul suggests a way to bring the two points of view together. Both Jesus and Paul seem to see the validity of both perspectives at issue, although it might seem to modern readers that both Jesus' disciples and those not being scrupulous about eating the meat had the better-developed theological perspectives.

Another complication in the life of faith is that our individual understandings of faith and its implications are not static. We are journeying toward a fuller understanding of who God is, who we are, and how we are becoming transformed. This is not to suggest that God is changing; rather it is our understandings about God that change. In fact, our ideas and understandings must change if we are to continue to grow. We are engaged in a learning process, and we cannot risk becoming so convinced that we are unable to attend to the call of God. Several weeks ago I heard a conference lay leader say, "That is not what I thought ten years ago, and ten years from now I may have a different view, but for now, this is the best I know." It struck me that if each of us recognized that this maturation process was occurring, we might be able to receive input more freely; in fact, we might seek it out.

In the face of this complex assortment of factors that could make our conclusions tentative and keep us from acting on them, we face a call to mission and ministry in the world. Once we hear and see the needs around us (for food, for justice, for a relationship with God), we must be able to respond with some assurance that this or that intervention promotes the cause of righteousness. We also are asked to come to conclusions about what the church believes or approves and to publish these conclusions for the edification of members and nonmembers.

Growth Requirements for Listening and Reflecting

Knowing that our understanding is partial, that we are continuing to grow, and that we need the input of the whole church to understand and speak the truth more fully, how can we formulate

our positions? I will suggest that this effort imposes several requirements. First, we need to be able to make connections across
theological and political spectrums with believers espousing a
variety of views. In the past few years, the informal United Methodist Dialogue group has seen that when someone shares the ways
in which a particular position relates to his or her own journey, we
begin to arrive at new understanding, getting past political presuppositions and engaging each other in a new way. It seems that we
need to experience the issues in the context of our several journeys in order to trust each other enough to be open to learn.

Second, we must be well grounded in why we think what we
think. This clarity is essential as our views are to be communicated
to others; and if our positions are to be heard and be instructive,
they must be understood. In addition, we must know and understand the premises and the context that shape our own positions
if we are to reflect on them for ourselves in the light of our
continued learning.

Third, we must form these views with enough humility to allow
us to listen to the learning and experience of others in order to
test our conclusions and flesh out our vision. This humility would
allow us to recognize that God is at work both in our own lives and
in the lives of others in the church and that we need the seasoning
of their experiences as well as our own. It would also allow us to
listen well. In order to grow as a community of faith, we must be
disciplined about listening first to understand the position/expe-
rience of others who are also on the journey. Once another's
position is understood, we can hold our own original position side
by side with the new view and evaluate them both. It is not enough
to evaluate or challenge the new view. The speakers should be
informing and teaching each other. This process of reflection and
refinement would honor the Christ in each one and add breadth
and depth to our views.

This is not to suggest that all honest seekers after truth are
without error, or that there are no beliefs or views that we cannot
adopt within the context of a United Methodist expression of
Christianity. However, the process of listening and reflecting may
result in new understandings, even if the positions in question
cannot be reconciled.

The Church's Teaching and Conciliar Roles

Of course, when the General Conference debates a theological statement, or when an annual conference or local church is debating about a particular position or course of action, the degree of ambiguity suggested here may be uncomfortable and may need to be resolved. In these instances we should consider the church in two roles. One is its teaching role. In this role the church focuses mainly on those of us who belong. We are concerned about nurturing, challenging, and guiding those people for whom the church provides a spiritual home. With respect to these people, the process itself is extremely important. The other role that bears consideration is a conciliar one in which the church takes positions and makes statements that are designed to be normative, or that affect and deal with people and situations outside the church. While "outsiders" may also be interested in the church's decision-making process, what is most likely at issue for them is the content of the position and how it supports or challenges their own position.

When the church is performing a conciliar function, the tension with the teaching function easily becomes evident. The process of evolving a statement tends to entrench us in our original views rather than expanding our understanding. We become focused on concluding the discussion. It is easy to lose sight of the individual faith journeys that are wrapped up in the process and progress of the decision; instead we are focused on the content of the proposition. We have speeches for and against. We make amendments. We put the matter to a vote. Then we consider the matter to be concluded, even if discontent is evident and the number in the minority or the number not voting is large.

The factors outlined above would suggest that we would be well served by reconsidering this process. Provision should be made for incorporating and respecting a diversity of opinion. This might mean that we would provide a variety of forums for discussing matters of importance in order to allow persons to absorb a wider spectrum of views. Perhaps major propositions could be introduced a day or so before the debate is to be concluded and conference members encouraged to seek out persons with concerns about the proposal. This might allow better decision making that would both represent and form the church.

General Conference Pronouncements like a Yellow Stripe

Perhaps it would also be helpful to think differently about the theological pronouncements of General Conference. What if we understood those pronouncements to be like the yellow stripe painted in the center of the road? Persons traveling far to the right or left of the stripe may still be on the road and, in fact, may still be being guided by the stripe. Certainly, there are also positions that are off the road, or that may be headed off the road. These must be guided by the unity on the essentials that is the prerequisite to this dialogue. However, all of the positions that are held by persons who are in agreement on the essentials and who are seeking to share their faith journey in the church should be heard. Some views may benefit from truly open exchange, and the open exchange may benefit the body. We need to find a way to permit the expressions of the variety of positions that are possible on the road and to discuss matters across a wide spectrum even after our own views have been stated or published.

In order to honor the Spirit of Christ working in us and the believers around us, and to act with the humility appropriate to a learner and the commitment of a disciple, we negotiate a delicate balance. We must seek to understand the things of God and to form conclusions about how God would have us act and react. We must live into these conclusions. That is to say, we do not exercise theological reflection merely from a desire to know, but also as a basis for action. Act we must, based on the best thinking and the best learning we can muster. But somehow we must manage to hold lightly to these conclusions, so that we can hear the testimony of others in whom God is also at work and be formed by the action of God in us and around us, looking forward to a day of completion. "For now we see in a mirror, dimly, but then we will see face to face. Now I know only in part; then I will know fully, even as I have been fully known" (1 Cor. 13:12).

Discovering Liberty in Nonessentials

Joy J. Moore

Can we discover liberty in nonessentials? Is there a freedom available to us that enhances our ability to be a transforming agent in society? Can we find a liberty that gives genuine freedom while preserving deep unity in the faith? Is liberty in nonessentials actually dependent on unity in essentials?

Diversity and Identity

When we think of nonessentials, we naturally think of issues of style, polity, and social concern. Compared to the reality of God, or the great verities of the faith like the Incarnation and Resurrection, these matters would appear to be in another league. Yet immediately we want to protest. Style, polity, and social concerns cannot be disregarded or set aside. So we need a distinction.

Essentials are tied to the basic concepts of our tradition; they spell out the *why* of the faith for us. Nonessentials are tied to the setting or context of the practice of our tradition; they focus on the *how* of the faith. Every community has its basic, determining concepts and convictions: its essentials. However, equally every community has myriad ways of expressing its faith: its nonessentials. If you like, it has a message, and it has ways of conveying that message in context. Both are crucial, for there is no community without a variety of expressions, no culture without variation in style, no message without different media of expression.

When I was growing up, we lived in the same house until I was seventeen. I attended the public elementary school, as did most of the other children in the neighborhood. Many of the teachers lived in the vicinity. The fundamentals of my surroundings remained the same, as I learned about the diversity of my community, my culture, and the manner of communication within it. Then we moved, and I became an itinerant. Mom bought another house, and I moved to college. I lived for a while in Europe, then left the city for the suburb. Then I left one state for another. In the spirit of the early circuit rider, I have moved around Michigan just enough to feel at home virtually anywhere in the lower peninsula.

As I picked up new addresses, I learned the culture of America. It is a dazzling array of diversity: suburbia; upper middle class; inner-city; poor white; generation X; African American. I discovered communities based on economics, on education, and on ethnicity. I have learned to communicate with the alphabet: UMS, COM, IRS, NAACP, UAW, IBM, BMW, TOYS-"R"-US. I have come to comprehend the language of feminists, the jargon of fundamentalists, and the foibles of four year olds.

Each group is part of the culture of North America. Within the larger picture, each group seeks to identify its distinctive ethos, its own horizon for understanding and defining its actions. As I moved from group to group, I struggled with my own identity and system of meaning. Some of my own experiences in these transitions were in conflict with my own deepest identity. Sometimes I experimented with options presented by others. I toyed with alternatives that were irrational but enjoyable leaps toward change, done for the sake of opportunity, self-expression, or rebellion. It is at once exhilarating and daunting to review and consider all the options that were available to me. The exposure and the journey have helped me to recognize who I am: undeniably female; unapologetically black; unashamedly Christian.

An Analogy with Music

Let us consider this question of self-identity for contemporary United Methodists. Should we try to find unity around our nonessentials? As we pursue this issue, think for a moment of the place of music in our lives. Music is an expression of the soul of society, signaling in part who we are as a community. "Give me the making of the songs of a nation, and I care not who writes its laws." In this epigram, the nineteenth-century Scottish political thinker, Andrew Fletcher, recognized where to discover the heart of a community. We acknowledge this when we recognize that popular music tells more about a generation than the ever-expanding legal treatise etched, exploited, and erased in the halls of its governing institutions.

Now, no one would eliminate music from a community, even though it is possible to conceive of the same community with different music or maybe (heaven forbid) without any music at all. Likewise, naming various practices or actions as nonessentials does not suggest an end to action. *How* we dwell together is as important as *that* we dwell together. Every family knows this as a living truth. Likewise, in United Methodism we operate in freedom, a freedom that calls us to express our unity through our diversity. To take an obvious example, our connectional system is pivotal to the ethos of United Methodism, to the way we express ourselves as a community. Yet, this is not what makes us "church." It is our particular way of being community, it is our inimitable way of expressing the unity of the church. It is the way we practice community together. Like music expresses the heart of a culture, whether rap, rock, country, or blues, so our polity of administrative boards, councils on ministries, agreed liturgies, or Korean-language services expresses the soul of our tradition. The essence of the tradition cannot be reduced to the medium, yet it is characteristically embodied and expressed in and through it. Just as there is more to music than the electricity of the medium, so there is more to the tradition than the nuts and bolts of polity. Yet the music comes to us through the medium, and the message of Christianity comes to us through the nuts and bolts of such mundane realities as boards and liturgies. Keeping this crucial distinction in place gives room for freedom; our passion for God and each other is free to be expressed in a great variety of ways.

There is a deep paradox here, which bears careful pondering. Unity and freedom are tied inextricably together. Being free to think, or speak, or act, is not the equivalent of having a vacuum between the ears. The mind thinks, speaks, and acts out of a rich body of thoughts, images, convictions, beliefs, and ideas. These are often thought to be limits; they are actually the lifeblood of our existence as complex persons. They constitute who we are; they provide the boundaries and horizons of our identity as persons. In a community, we possess shared values, collective motivations, joint convictions, and common standards that identify who we are. To outsiders, they will appear as limits. But these limits are actually our liberator, setting a point of departure, a frame of reference, and a recognizable destination. Without some accepted point of reference, the gift of freedom becomes the Trojan horse of a tradition. It introduces foreign agents and material that destroy the tradition from within. Yet properly rooted and grounded, the gift of freedom is essential to the creativity and vitality of the tradition.

Consider again the analogy with music. Music is composed of certain tones, rhythm, melody, and harmony. All music is sound, but not all sound is music. The sound of a hammer can have a rhythm; a trained ear might recognize its tone. Nevertheless, the sound of a hammer does not represent music. Moreover, once the essentials of music have been learned, endlessly debating the established descriptions of music will not liberate aspiring musicians. Indeed, such debate generally distracts from potential performance or transforms it into an exercise in semantic gymnastics. Nobody wants to listen to semantic exercises when they go to a concert. Yet the common definitions and descriptions cannot be ignored or set aside. They are not a form of bondage; they are not even limits to our freedom. They make it possible for the offered sound to be recognized as music.

Diversity, Goodwill, and Unity

It is easy to be confused at this juncture. Change in structure, or in financial and personnel resources, or in polity, is taken as a change in the identity of the community. Changes in the means of operation, however, do not mean that the operation itself is abandoned. We inevitably have to adjust structures due to all sorts of pressures, even if we do not understand why. But change in these matters does not erase the fundamental identity of the community. Furthermore, differences of style or expression are sometimes taken as differences in basic agenda. We meet someone who belongs to a different caucus and we are suspicious. Our behavior too often reflects that of bigots who hold stereotypes against persons of a different ethnicity. Our labels assist us in practicing prejudiced segregation. Are conservatives really racist, progress-resistant good ol' boys, reaching for the restoration of the rights of privilege for white male clergy? Is the Good News caucus a group of right-wing religious fanatics who undermine *The Book of Discipline* by upholding orthodoxy? Are liberals those who maintain their own status quo by speaking loudly of liberty and justice and by identifying these with the interests of representative constituencies rather than with the interests of believers in Jesus Christ? We need to examine how we depict each other in the light of the distinction between essentials and nonessentials.

Another temptation arises here: the temptation to misread what we are as a community. We are indeed diverse, even pluralistic. But is our diversity misconstrued when the middle class is taken to mean Methodism, UMCOR to mean mission, practicing homosexuals to mean the oppressed, COSROW to mean women, children to mean the Christian education program, EMLC to mean urban ministry, and the UMW to mean the church? When this happens, United Methodists have forgotten that the church exists as a unique community, as a called-out people who are responding to a unique story. Diversity has been transformed into something grander than it really is.

Diversity has nothing to do with naming oppression and victimization. To be diverse simply means to be different, to possess different abilities, to have a different focus, to undergo different experiences. Diversity does not carry judgment with it. Neither does the word *multicultural*. To be multicultural means that one has the ability to see from another perspective or to recognize that the world is not identical to my own sphere of experience. Such an outlook is crucial to genuine freedom. It enables us to move beyond the limits of gender, race, or class. By being diverse and multicultural we are liberated to encounter the infinite expression of a shared identity in Christ. We tell our own diverse stories or we identify our own unique cultures, not to highlight what civil rights or our social agendas have afforded us, but to honor the God who sought us and formed us to be a community together.

91

Diversity, rightly understood and applied, exalts our unity in Jesus Christ through the working of the Holy Spirit and to the great glory of God.

Without this unity, diversity becomes the occasion for a false individualism. Within the body, within the framework of the accepted unity of the whole, each part discovers the freedom to express its own style. The boundaries of firm foundations and the stability of a common story provide an arena in which we can grow personally and in which we can develop our individuality. Equally, the boundaries provide the foundations for being in but not of our secular and sometimes pagan culture. The society we currently inhabit is a cultural tapestry, not unlike many of the communities described in Scripture. However, right in the midst of the financial, political, sexual, and theological temptations of this world, a community has been identified and formed because of the resurrection of Jesus Christ. At times the tension between the church and the culture is so acute that it calls for an "in your face" stance against the dominant culture. This requires an allegiance to a Power outside ourselves that is above the social and political order. It requires also a corporate allegiance, a standing together, lest we be picked off one by one by the forces at work in the culture. So unity at one and the same time protects individuality and makes possible the healing of the nations.

Allegiance and Exploration

Our common allegiance is to God, who comes to meet us in divine revelation. Even our seeking is an expression of God's reaching out to find us through the working of the Holy Spirit in prevenient grace. Even before we seek God's face, God calls us. The initiative is with God from the beginning. God seeks us out. God reveals God's nature to us. By repentance and faith, by struggle and discovery, in adoration and joy, we find a new identity in God's Son, Jesus Christ. Our identity is not the expression of individual experience or of this or that interest group; it is the expression of our status as the very children of God, adopted by grace into a new community. Our agenda is not an agenda we have dreamed up for ourselves or borrowed from this or that group; it

92

is given by God as God calls us into the values of a new age on earth, which will be consummated in heaven. Owning this identity and embracing God's agenda, we invite all humanity to explore the creative and redemptive activity of God made known in Jesus Christ through the working of the Holy Spirit. Rather than promote ethnic and gender communities, we affirm and celebrate the testimony of all who proclaim a countercultural power of transformation in Jesus Christ. As a result of our baptism we bear the name of God rather than the name of our gender, race, and class. No longer identified by culture, human heritage, or economic status, our community is established by a common confession that Jesus Christ is Lord. The beauty and wonder of this new identity is that it is open to all regardless of gender, status, ethnicity, or nationality. This message can be shared by all, with all, and for all.

As we grow into and develop within this common identity, we readily draw on our reason and our experience. We explore who we are in part by investigating the fund of ideas, images, insights, and experiences that are inescapably our own. This is natural and human. Yet, if this were all we had to go on, there would be no hope of finding answers to the basic issues of meaning and significance. Happily, we know another source of knowledge which comes as a great gift from God as we receive our new identity in Christ. We are given divine revelation. It is at this point that the Bible enters the picture. Scripture depicts us not as agents seeking God but as lost sheep scattered and confused on the hillside. It is God who seeks us out and binds us together in Christ. Therein we are given our true story and an identity that unites us. From Adam to Mary, from Israel to the church, God is calling a people.

Our primary community of accountability is, therefore, the church of Jesus Christ. We belong to and with those persons who have surrendered their will to Jesus and seek his power to live lives of discipline, self-control, and integrity. This has at least two important implications. On the one hand, the community cannot but find suspect anyone or any organization that claims accountability to anyone other than God or any authority other than that of Scripture. There is an inescapable vertical relationship here which governs the life of the community from above. On the other hand, our horizontal relationships help us to be accountable to

God. We provoke one another to love and good works. Even more, these relationships, when rightly approached, help us to unpack the extraordinary treasures of grace given to us in divine revelation in the church. But when gender, nationality, race, employment, marital status, or anything else call into question God's Word, nonessentials have become essentials, and this shift in identity erodes the right use of tradition, reason, and the experience of the historic church.

It is only as we keep in mind the essentials that we are empowered truly to express our unique experiences. We receive the story given to us by God in the church. I may tell the story in rap. You may perform it through Bach. Some will quote the KJV; others prefer to work from the original Hebrew and Greek. As members of the church, all of us desire to express our faith in action. Here again we encounter our diversity. To change our world for the better we have to categorize. We have to break things down to understand them and remake them aright. Putting them back together in the right way is far from easy. When, at some point, we try to reassemble the fragments in our minds, we get overwhelmed. We should be. It is like trying to reassemble the fragments of a shattered mirror in order to see a true reflection. It is impossible; the distorted result is useless. Scripture destroys the illusion that the world is created of separate, unrelated forces. It calls us to gather the whole world, each person created in the image of God, as disciples of Jesus Christ. Then, collectively, we recognize a shared identity. We become the one Body of Christ, the church, God's instrument.

Singing Our Songs in the Household of Faith

Our music analogy is once again helpful as we think about the process of transforming the world. A musician will not tune a guitar to an out-of-tune piano. The church provides another alternative for tuning human hearts. Once tuned to the divine music of the gospel, we experience liberty and freedom to be all that God destined us to be. Our liberty is beyond the limitations of social order, psychological research, and political correctness. We sing a story of being called home after traveling the world. We come under the roof of God's house, acquiring new foundations and receiving a new name. Living in God's mansions does not mean that we stay at home all the time. On the contrary, we are sent out into the world to participate in its healing and redemption. In doing so we encounter other buildings, other stories, other communities. Some of us are tempted to switch homes, but this is only a temporary state if we have our wits about us. The more appropriate response to this kind of exposure is to remember who we are and whose we are. We use the occasion to name ourselves again as belonging to the household of God.

We have now migrated back to a point we touched on earlier. Going home to my childhood neighborhood takes me back to remember who I am. When I enter the old house I am grateful for the stable foundations. I recall with appreciation the wise ones I came to know in the area. It was because of the stability of the home and the wisdom of the neighbors that I learned how to express myself. My freedom was inextricably tied to those foundations and that wisdom of the ages. It is like that in the church, too. From time to time we go back and remember who we are. We look again at the foundations and seek out afresh the wisdom of those who were in the neighborhood. We remember who we are, we reclaim the meaning of our lives together, and we re-own our mission. As we journey back in time we find at the base of our history an ancient text, Holy Scripture. It has amazing contemporary relevance, so we examine it carefully. We look also at a not-so-ancient text, *The Book of Discipline,* and we explore its proposals. We quickly rediscover that United Methodism as part of the church universal is a connectional, countercultural community created through the Incarnation. We are the Body of Christ, a building not made with hands, whose foundations reach into heaven itself.

It is misleading to think that freedom consists in tearing the old place apart and starting all over again. To be sure, we can add a room here or there; or we can redecorate to our heart's content. Most certainly we will want to add a piano. However, even if we desired to do so, we cannot unhinge the foundations of the church, for they stand secure forever in the Word and grace of God. True freedom is found in acknowledging that we belong to the household of God. Exposed afresh to our heritage, we recognize anew who and what we are: undeniably Wesleyan, unapologetically united, and unashamedly Christian.

STUDY GUIDE

In two quite different essays, the issue of discovering liberty in nonessentials is explored. Harriett J. Olson struggles with the problem of reconciling individual liberty of conscience with keeping faith with United Methodism's teaching and practice. Neither Jesus nor Paul insisted that the same practices be observed by all believers in regard to fasting and eating meat. In our theological journeys, individual decisions must affect and be affected by our church connection. To encourage growth in grace and maturity, and because all knowledge is partial, broad dialogue appears imperative across theological and political spectrums, manifesting humility that permits listening and learning from the experiences of others. Act we must on the best that we know, but open to change as God leads us to new understanding.

Joy J. Moore contends essentials are tied to the basic conceptions of Christian tradition, while nonessentials are connected to how we live out or express this faith. United Methodists operate with a freedom that calls us to express our unity through our diversity. Limits, however, exist and serve as our liberators. She warns against stereotyping other Christians, but she expresses reservations whether every type of diversity is compatible with Christianity. Our identity as a people, the church of Jesus Christ, transcends individual gender, race, and class characteristics and commitments.

Items for Reflection

1. How do Christians reconcile the differences when the official teachings of their church conflict with their liberty of conscience? Imagine some historical times when this may have been true or some current issues that create dilemmas of conscience.

2. What criteria should be used in determining what is "essential" and "nonessential" to Christian belief and practice?

3. Are nonessentials only matters of style and polity or can they also include questions of theology and social concern? What would it mean to be a "conscientious objector" to certain church teachings?

4. Using the image of the "household of God," how much freedom to Christians have in rearranging the furniture of faith, adding new rooms to enhance diversity, or redecorating the theological landscape?

5. Imagine and discuss what might happen if United Methodists understood the church's theological pronouncements like a "yellow strip painted in the center of the road," guiding but not totally restricting faith and practice.

4

Desiring Charity in All Things

Maxie D. Dunnam

The disciples had been with Jesus for some time. They had seen him heal and perform other miracles. They had listened to his teaching to different audiences, and had shared intimate moments of conversation with him. They had observed him in public and private. So, one day Jesus asked them, "Who do people say that the Son of Man is?" (Matt. 16:13). They responded with what they had heard: "Some say John the Baptist, but others Elijah, and still others Jeremiah or one of the prophets" (Matt. 16:14).

Jesus pressed the question. He wanted their thoughts, their personal judgment: "But who do you say that I am?" Peter, speaking for the group, responded, "You are the Messiah, the Son of the living God" (vv. 15-16).

All three synoptic Gospels, Matthew, Mark, and Luke, record this encounter, and through the ages since, the church has seen this as a pivotal moment of revelation and teaching. On their testimony concerning who he was, Jesus said, "I will build my church, and the gates of Hades will not prevail against it" (v. 18).

Jesus Is Lord

For years, the simple, but profound and encompassing creed "Jesus is Lord" was the essence of the church's profession of faith. It is still the essence. I mean by essence what the dictionary says: "That which makes something what it is; the distinctive quality or qualities of something." That which makes the church what it is—the distinctive quality—is our confession and profession of Jesus Christ; who he is, what he has done for us, and the promise of salvation he makes to all humankind. There is no Christian church apart from Jesus Christ. There is no Christian history apart from persons encountering Jesus Christ, confessing and professing faith in him.

Knowing who Jesus is involves divine revelation rather than human assessment alone. Christianity is not just a confession, it is a *profession* of faith. Faith is a gift of God, but our profession is not a groundless assertion. It arises out of the witness of Scripture and out of the experience of persons with Jesus. It is interesting that in all three Gospels where this confession of the Messiah is recorded, Jesus warned them not to tell anyone. A lot of discussion has surrounded that part of the story. Whatever else is involved, this much is clear: the full nature of the Messiah was not yet understood, not even by the disciples. In Luke's account this is made clear:

> Jesus strictly warned them not to tell this to anyone. And he said, "The Son of Man must suffer many things and be rejected by the elders, chief priests and teachers of the law, and he must be killed and on the third day be raised to life." (9:21-22 NIV)

At the point of the revelation in Caesarea, the disciples were becoming aware of Jesus being more than a man; more than Elijah or one of the prophets, with a far more crucial role to play in God's plan and purpose, Jesus was the Son of Man, the Messiah. But there was more to be revealed and experienced: Jesus was the Son of the living God, and as he told them, his death and resurrection would reveal the rest of the story.

A Rigid Fundamentalism

For years United Methodism has wrestled with this part of the slogan being discussed in these essays: "In essentials, unity; in non-essentials, liberty; and, in all things, charity." Implicitly, we have forgotten—if not forgotten, then certainly neglected—the hinge element of the "slogan": *essentials. Liberty* and *charity* have become a rigid "fundamentalism," the watchwords of condemnation against those who contend that we must recover a commitment to the essentials.

This fundamentalism of liberty and charity was inadvertently institutionalized by the General Conference in 1972. We made doctrinal pluralism the center around which we ordered our life as a denomination. What happened, in fact, was that pluralism became an ideology garnering more attention and commitment than doctrine or theology. For two decades "in non-essentials, liberty, and, in all things, charity" has been reduced to a hyper-toleration in which even raising the question of "essentials" is seen as intolerance that has no place in United Methodism.

To have charity in all things does not mean an unexamined and unquestioned commitment to pluralism and diversity. It means that we begin at the center—Jesus Christ as Son of God, Savior, and Lord—and from that center we diligently seek to order our life as a unique community that stands against the moral relativism that is the cancer of our age. Charity must be defined with reference to God's highest expression of love in sending his Son to live among us, and die for our salvation. We value diversity, but do not make diversity redemptive in itself. While "inclusivity," with respect to culture and race are clearly Christian, and by contrast "exclusivity" must be clearly rejected on Christian principles, this does not mean that we sacrifice truth claims for the sake of "getting along together," especially when it is truth claims about Jesus that give us life and are the ordering dynamics of Christian community. Where truth is concerned, falsehood and error must be excluded, regardless of culture or race. Truth by its very nature is exclusive. To be sure, our insights may be partial, and many facets of truth are needed for wholeness. But, in the Christian view of reality, everyone's well-being consists in acknowledging Christ as he truly is, accepting him as Savior and Lord, obeying his commands, being a part of the community of which he is the head, and bringing others to faith in him. We do not promote the well-being of others if we do not uphold the truth they themselves need. John Wesley based his call to love (charity) on the love that God gave us in Jesus Christ. "It behooves us therefore to examine well upon what foundation our love of neighbor stands: whether it is really built upon the love of God; whether 'we' do 'love because He first loved us' " (Sermon 23, part I, section 1). He insisted that the love Christians know and share is the love of Christ flowing through

100

them. A church in which charity of that sort "in all things" dwells will be a vibrant fellowship of acceptance where persons live together with different opinions, celebrate the pursuit of truth, submit themselves to the Lordship of Christ and the authority of Scripture, and give themselves sacrificially to Christ's redemptive mission of service to the world. Our worship of God, as we know God in Christ, keeps our identity clear. Our ministry to each other and to the world in Christ's name is the dynamic bonding that keeps us alive as a part of the church—the Body of Christ.

The Heretical Imperative

That we were on the wrong path as a denomination with our hypertoleration and our superficial, unexamined commitment to pluralism has been recognized for some time. In his Episcopal Address at the General Conference in 1984, Bishop Jack M. Tuell said, "The time has come to say the last rites over the notion that the defining characteristic of United Methodist theology is pluralism. The word [pluralism] may have some descriptive value, but it has no defining value. It carries philosophic overtones which contradict our understanding of the Christian faith." I think the bishop was right.

Peter Berger speaks about the "heretical imperative," that is the necessity to choose a religious faith, or to choose not to have one. Berger says "this heretical imperative is the endemic challenge that issues from a pluralistic society." I do not believe I'm violating Berger's thought when I suggest that the "heretical imperative" within the Christian family is centered not on whether we will choose a religious faith or not—but what we choose to believe about Jesus Christ: his incarnation, his life and ministry, his death and resurrection, his redemption, his triumph in the kingdom, our salvation and sanctification through him, his living presence among us and within us through the Holy Spirit as the power to be and do all God calls us to be and do.

In the *Christian Century* Thomas Oden and Lewis Mudge recently debated the issue of "heresy."[1] In his response to Oden, who pleads for us to recognize that heresy is abroad in our church, and especially in our seminaries, Mudge called for a "gathering around the center." In his counterresponse to Mudge, Oden asks, "Can there be a center without a circumference?" This is not a play on words. That's the reason the debate is so crucial. The center has to be more clearly designated and defined because the center will fashion the circumference. That is what some are seeking to do in the Confessing Movement. The affirmation of the movement is not a creed to replace or even to be added to what we already have in the *Discipline* of our church, but it is a call to the church to confess with one voice Jesus Christ as Son, Savior, and Lord. This is the center around which we are to move in faith and doctrine.

This is where I would disagree heartily with Lewis Mudge. He says: "Who is in the position to define what is 'heretical?' Our situation today is that no one stands in the center. No one has the right to arrogate to himself or herself a definitive status. We need to determine together where the center is. No literal repetition of formulas coming from any particular place or time in the history of the church can help us now."[2]

Mudge is right when he says, "No one has the right to arrogate to himself or herself the definitive status," but what about his claim that no "formulas coming from any particular place or time in the history of the church can help us now"? What does this say about the church as "the people of God"?—the church that is a part of God's history? In his first epistle, Peter used the titles applied to Israel to describe the church; he called us a "chosen race, a royal priesthood, a holy nation, God's own people" (1 Pet. 2:9). I do not believe that those who are contending for an adherence to, for instance, the Nicene Creed, are arrogating to themselves definitive status. They are claiming the wisdom of "the people of God." They are seeking to begin a dialogue not to determine where the center is, but to claim the center that has already been determined by the church. We are simply calling for an adherence to Scripture and the classic creeds that have defined our life as Christians, and are the expression of Christian consensus. We are contending that Scripture is our final authority and that Jesus Christ, as the Son of God, Savior, and Lord, is the center that defines the circumference.

What, then, does "in all things, charity" mean? It does not mean what we have sought to make it mean during the past twenty years—a hypertoleration and a mindless, superficial pluralism. It does not mean we can badger others and settle all issues by accusing others of exclusivity and claiming inclusivity as the final warrant of love. It means that we do not set out to find unity in diversity. We begin by claiming our unity in Jesus Christ, and we celebrate the diversity in the community Christ creates.

The following assertions will help us wrestle with the issue of unity, liberty, and charity.

No Church Apart from Jesus

There is no Christian church apart from Jesus Christ, no Christian community apart from some personal experience of him. The church is the Body of Christ. What we think of Jesus Christ not only makes the biggest difference in our lives, but also the nature and life of the church is determined by Jesus Christ—who he is, what he did, and what he does. Naturally, our personal experience of Jesus cannot be disconnected from what we think of him. That makes even more crucial what the church through the ages has said about him. Who Jesus is defines and informs our experience of him.

Integrity at Center—Ambiguity at Circumference

If there is integrity at the center, that is, where our Christology is concerned, then there can be ambiguity at the circumference. That doesn't mean there are no boundaries; there are. Our primary source for the setting of these boundaries is Scripture, with the additional aid of reason, tradition, and experience. Our problems come when we seek to move the center to some point out at the circumference field.

The question arises, of course, how do we deal with the ambiguity? I propose that we make more use of what recent Roman Catholic thought is calling for: focusing on "the sense of the faithful." Richard J. Mouw has introduced this dynamic in his challenging book *Consulting the Faithful.* He says:

The disdain many Christian scholars show toward domestic popular religious culture is itself a theological defect, stemming from a failure to develop an adequate theological understanding of ordinary religious people.

The notion that the laity's perspective should be taken into account in assessing a theological or ethical teaching is not entirely new to Catholic theology, but in the past the laity was assigned a fairly passive role in the theological formulation. Cardinal Newman was signaling a new emphasis on the laity's active role in the process when he wrote in the nineteenth century that church leaders must take seriously "a sort of instinct, . . . deep in the bosom of the mystical body of Christ."[3]

It is commendable that all the leaders of the church—pastors, bishops, heads of boards and agencies, seminaries and even caucus groups—champion the priesthood of all believers. The Bishops' report on ministry and the Board of Discipleship's report on baptism, two big issues before the 1996 General Conference, give a central place to the *laos,* the whole people of God. But how much attention are these leaders willing to give to the "instincts" of the laity? How much attention to the "sense of the faithful" as it relates to matters such as abortion and the ordination of practicing homosexuals? How much freedom will we give laypersons in choosing the mission expression of their local congregations and how they prioritize their spending? Will voices who get a hearing in seminaries, national meetings, and the Methodist press not be at least questioned, if not checked, by our leaders when they accuse lay Christians of homophobia and patriarchy when these laypersons are being faithful to their understanding of Scripture, and especially when they are in harmony with the *Discipline* of United Methodism and with the majority of Christians around the world?

If we are going to have charity in all things, then certainly those who are a part of the General Conference should think long and hard about action that clearly violates the "sense of the faithful." Charity in all things allows ambiguity at the circumference, but does not allow church leadership to advocate, much less impose on the church as a whole, that which is so far from the *center* that, to accept it, would demand a spiritual and moral elasticity beyond the capacity of the faithful.

This does not mean that truth and moral issues can be determined by majority vote. It is simply a plea that the General Conference collect the wisdom of the whole church and enter into theological reflection, using reason and experience, yet staying faithful to those truths that constitutionally the General Conference has said it cannot change, that is, the twenty-five Articles and the Confession of Faith.

The Church—Place of Hospitality

I believe that the church, as the Body of Christ, the fellowship of which Christ is the head, is a home of grace. As a home of grace, it is a place of hospitality and a home for all. If it is not a home for all, it is not a home at all. By nature, if it is Christian, the church is redemptive and transforming. Though some may choose not to be a part of the Christian community because of the community's call to new life in Christ, the church is not to be faulted. As Wesley would put it, grace may be universally offered though not universally received. It is tragic when any community that calls itself Christian is so amorphous in its doctrine and teaching that there are no distinctive faith commitments called for. Equally tragic, perhaps more so, is for the church to be so "accepting" of all moral behavior and failure that persons are never confronted with sin and/or offered the redemptive transforming grace of Jesus Christ. "In all things, charity" means that because the church is the home of grace, it receives all as they are and where they are, depending on the grace of Jesus Christ never to leave us as we are or where we are.

Heresy

If there is an absolute center, which classic Christianity says there is, then there is going to be practical and theoretical heresy. There are going to be those who refute the "center," and offer an alternative. That has been true throughout Christian history, and the church has always refuted the "optional" teaching. There will always be those who refuse to accept the center, Jesus Christ, as the eternal Son of God incarnate, as God's self-revelation, as God's offer of salvation to all humankind, as the pattern of life to which we are called, and as sender of the Spirit who makes us "new creatures." "In all things, charity" does not mean that the church can forget the center and not challenge those who propose a more culturally acceptable expression of the gospel. In "An Open Letter to Presbyterians: Theological Analysis of Issues raised by the Re-Imagining Conference," six professors from Princeton Theological Seminary said:

> The unity of the Church is not endangered when heresies are labeled as such. On the contrary, the unity of the Church is a unity in its Head, Jesus Christ, who is the fullness of wisdom and truth. It is not those who point out the heresy and apostasy of others who break that unity. It is rather the heretic and the apostate who break the unity of the Church by undermining the Church's obedience to its Head. Those who raise the necessary protest are simply bringing to the light of day the fact that the unity of the Church has already been shattered.

Desiring charity in all things for the church means that we order our love around the only unity that will enable us to have and celebrate diversity in the church. It is the unity created by our acceptance of God's gift of God's self in his Son, Jesus Christ, to be our Savior and Lord.

NOTES

1. Thomas Oden and Lewis Mudge, *Christian Century,* April 12, 1995.
2. Ibid., p. 393.
3. Richard J. Mouw, *Consulting the Faithful: What Christian Intellectuals Can Learn from Popular Religion* (Grand Rapids: Wm. B. Eerdmans Publishing Co., 1994), p. 23.

Desiring Charity in All Things

Justo L. González

A Hymn That Will Not Let Me Go

It has been noted that for most Christians, no matter what we might say or think, the hymns we sing and the words we memorize in worship are at least as important—and usually more important—than any doctrinal statement. Indeed, many of us, when we are sorely tried or distressed and feel the need to go to the deepest resources of our faith, do not go to a sermon we heard or to a book we read, but rather to a hymn we have sung repeatedly, or to a verse or psalm we memorized as children. Furthermore, in spite of what some theologians and authors might think or hope, our belief system is shaped more by our worship and devotional experiences than by theological argument or doctrinal statement. This is a phenomenon to which historians of doctrine refer as *lex orandi est lex credendi*—the rule or practice of worship is the rule or practice of belief. And that is as it should be, for after all, what makes the church the church is not its doctrines—and much less its organization—as much as its experience of worship. Thus, for instance, the church was worshiping Jesus as God long before it felt compelled to issue doctrinal statements declaring that Jesus is God, and trying to explain how that can be.

Concretely, this means that all of us have experiences of worship and devotion that have profoundly shaped our lives and theology, and which we must acknowledge if we are to understand that theology.

In my case, one of those experiences is intimately connected with George Matheson's famous hymn, "O Love That Wilt Not Let Me Go." It was my father's favorite hymn. One of his novels, which

I read as a youth, ended with that hymn. Since my father served as a tent-making minister in a small rural church, and I attended there with him on weekends, we sang that hymn at least once a month—and probably much more than that. Like me, my father couldn't carry a tune; but I remember sitting as a child in a clearing in the woods and hearing him approaching, humming softly what, with some effort, I could recognize as this hymn.

I also remember thinking how fortunate I was that my parents were firm believers in this Love that would not let them go, for it also meant that their love would not let me go. My mother used to speak of the time when my father was in prison during a revolution, when my older brother was still a toddler, and how what sustained her during those difficult times was this Love that would not let her go.

For all these reasons, whenever I think of God, I think first of all of this Love that will not let me go, much as my parents' love would not let me go.

A Love That Lets Go

And yet, that is only one side of love. True love does let go. My parents held my hand as I took my first steps; but then they let me go, even knowing that I would stumble and fall, because true love required that I be allowed to learn how to walk on my own two feet. Because they loved me, they had to let me go! They let go of my hand and let me try to walk and even stumble, precisely because in another sense their love would not let go!

As I have grown up and matured in my understanding of the faith, I have come to see that the same is true of God's love. This is a common theme of the parables of Jesus that we usually call "parables of stewardship." Many of them begin with the story of the principal actor (the owner of the vineyard, a ruler, the master of a household, the rich man who gave the talents to his servants) going away "to a distant country." It is while that person is away that those left behind have the opportunity to exercise their stewardship. Thus, in a sense, the parables of stewardship are parables of absence. They are parables about what to do in a situation in which God has given us space to be responsible, how to act when God's love—like my parents' love—lets us go.

It is true that as Christians we are always held in the hand of God, whose love will never let us go. But it is also true that we live in a world that does not acknowledge that love—that refuses to live by that love.

Love Is No Hiding Place

Most of us have—all of us should have—memories of love as a hiding place, as a place of safety amid the perils and pains of life. Those are the memories of safety in our mother's bosom, of protection under our father's arm, of faith that carried us through times of storm and stress. We probably also have memories of times when the church, the community of faith, has provided that safe place that we so sorely needed in the midst of the turmoils and pains of life.

Yet we must also know that the purpose of a parent's love is not to provide false protection against the realities of the world, but rather to prepare us for living in that world. And if, as is clearly God's case, that parent also loves the whole world, this means that we must not hide behind our own personal experience of love in order not to deal with the world.

There are many ways we use love as a hiding place. One such way is to use love as an excuse not to confront persons or situations that need to be confronted. One of my first experiences of racism in this country was a meeting in which a problem was being discussed. I offered a suggestion, and it was ignored. Two minutes later, another person, a white man, offered the same solution, and it was immediately adopted by the majority. It was clear to me that they had not even heard what I had said—that before I even began to speak they were discounting anything I had to say. These were very nice, loving Christian people who would have been very surprised, and probably even hurt, had I told them that I perceived a racist attitude in their behavior. I decided that the loving thing to do was to remain silent. Today I know that I was hiding behind the excuse of love, that by not confronting them I was really telling myself that if my opinion did not count for them, theirs would not count for me. I decided to ignore them, and I called that love!

Desiring Love in All Things

There is, however, another way in which we use love as an excuse or a hiding place. That is by being unwittingly selective about those things where love applies. Probably the most difficult part of "in all things, charity" is not the second half of the dictum, to desire charity, but the first—*in all things*. It is much easier for us to see what love or charity requires when it does not challenge us than when it does.

This is particularly true of unequal relationships. In such relationships, quite often one side claims to speak for justice, and the other takes on the mantle of love. I saw this at work in a meeting of leaders of a denomination that does not ordain women. A nun was arguing for the equality of women in the church, and consequently, for their ordination. A priest responded that the sister should not be so angry, but must be more loving. Listening to the dialogue, I observed that the priest was just as angry as the nun, and that she in turn was angry because she loved this church that did not recognize her as an equal. The priest was saying that the nun must practice charity in all things, even in accepting her own oppression; but he did not see the need to practice charity in acknowledging the issue of justice in the nun's argument.

This is typical of many of our struggles in the church today. Those who can count on the support of tradition, power, or privilege are ready to see the lack of charity of those who challenge them. They call their opponents to "desire charity in all things." Thus for many of those who do not stand at the center of power or privilege, to "desire charity" is a code word for not changing anything. We see this often in the local church, where the youth are often told to be more loving, while many adults do not take the time to try to understand what the youth are saying. We also see it at more general levels of church life, where "in all things, charity" is often used as a way to stifle the protest of some who have every right to protest.

This was clear to some of the early Christian writers who dealt with the relationship between charity and justice. Ambrose, for instance, who lived in Milan in the fourth century, analyzed both concepts,[1] justice and charity. Justice was a very important category for Roman society, and one of the pillars of Roman law. Charity was clearly important for Christians. In Ambrose's time, many Christians apparently drew their understanding of justice from Roman law and their view of charity and love from the gospel, and they kept the two isolated from each other. But Ambrose—and most Christian teachers with him—declared that the gospel required that the Roman notion of justice be corrected at least on two scores:

First, "they say that the first expression of justice is, to hurt no one, except when driven to it by wrongs received." This is clearly against the gospel of Jesus, "who came to give grace, not to bring harm." In other words, Christians cannot hide behind a legal understanding of justice in order not to act in the loving fashion that the gospel requires of them.

Second, says Ambrose, "they considered it consonant with justice that one should treat common, that is, public property as public, and private as private." Again, this was one of the pillars of Roman law, which was basically property law. But Ambrose goes on to say that much that is considered private—including private privileges—is often used in an unjust manner. These things, no matter by whom held, are intended for the good of all, and to use them for one's own good alone is not consonant with a Christian understanding of justice. Although in this passage Ambrose is dealing directly with property, we can extend his argument to all sorts of privilege and power. They are given not so that those who have them might enjoy them, but so that we may share them in love and charity.

Ambrose's conclusion is that the pagans' main error is to treat justice and charity as two separate things, when in fact the two are interconnected. They are so tightly wound, says Ambrose, that one cannot even begin to practice charity without first doing justice, and that justice without charity is injustice. In the case of money, which is Ambrose's subject in this context, this would mean, for instance, that a Christian who pays unjust wages cannot claim that feeding a hungry employee is an act of charity. At best, it is an act of partial justice—and even then it is not enough.

Since most of the debates in the church today have to do with other issues, it may be well to reflect on what this connection between charity and justice might mean in those other contexts.

Think for instance of the case of the nun and the priest. Consider first the nun. She is clearly calling for justice. What does charity require of her so that her call may be a genuine call to Christian justice? Consider then the priest. He is asking for more love and charity. What would be required of him—and his church—so that his call to love may be based on justice? What would it mean for each of them, to seek charity in *all* things?

Or think of me sitting in that committee. I hid behind love and said nothing. If I had understood that love requires justice, what would I have done differently? If I had confronted my colleagues with their hidden racism, how could they have reacted? Which of their possible reactions would manifest their desire to seek charity in *all* things?

Finally, think of situations that evoke bitter confrontation between yourself and others in the church. What would be required of you were you to desire charity in *all* things—even in those matters where you do not perceive an issue of justice, but others do?

A Love That Will Not Let Us Go!

We might not like the answers to the questions just posed. They might require of us more than we are willing to give or to do. And yet, in this sense also God's love will not let us go! My parents' love would not let me go, not only in the sense that they always sought what was best for me, but also in the sense that they would not let me get away with mischief. Likewise, for those of us who claim the name of Christ, these are not optional matters that we may take or leave. As we claim God's love, we also accept the claim of that love on us.

Then, the Love that will not let us go also shows us the pattern for the love or charity that is required of us. It too must be a love that does not let go, that does not easily give up, that is in it "for the long haul." I do not know what I should have said in that committee meeting. Nor do I know what the priest ought to have said to the nun. But I do know that if we are to find solutions to these matters we must not hope to do it quickly or cheaply. No matter what I had done at that committee, or what the priest might have said, it would have been only the beginning of a long process. The Love to which I sing "seekest me through pain." It is the Love of the cross, and of the centuries of preparation for the cross, and of the centuries of follow-up on the cross, and of my rising every time—oh, so many times!—I have fallen.

Finally, the Love that will not let us go is also a guarantee that, even if and when we are right, we do not have to win every argument. We do not have to be proved right. We do not have to silence or crush the enemy. It is a Love on which I can "rest my weary soul," a Light to which I can "yield my flickering torch," a Joy "that seekest me through pain," a Cross "that liftest up my head." Resting on that Love—and resting only on that Love—we can truly, sincerely, and jointly desire "in all things, charity."

NOTE

1. What follows is a summary of his argument in a number of his works, especially in *Duties of the Clergy,* book 2, chaps. 28–36. See also Justo L. González, *Faith and Wealth* (San Francisco: HarperCollins, 1990), pp. 187-93.

STUDY GUIDE

Both authors concur that desiring "in all things, charity" does not mean unconditional acceptance of everything. Where they would draw the lines, however, would be dramatically different. Both accent the primacy of love or grace, but the tone and topics they address are remarkably different.

Maxie D. Dunnam argues that charity or love does not mean unquestioned commitment to theological pluralism or acceptance of all human behavior. Unity is not in diversity per se, but unity is in Jesus Christ as Lord, and "we celebrate the diversity in the community Christ creates." Charity allows some ambiguity at the circumference, but only when centrality of Christ is affirmed. The grace offered is not simply accepting, but is redemptive and transforming.

Justo L. González de-emphasizes doctrine, suggesting that worship, devotion, and hymn singing have a more prominent role in shaping faith and the church. Emphasizing the centrality of love in our understanding of God, he, however, expresses concern that desiring "in all things, charity" can sometimes mean hiding from genuine love. Highlighting the interconnection between justice and love, he demonstrates how love can obscure racism, oppression, and injustice. Practicing charity without justice or justice without charity is impossible for Christians.

Items for Reflection

1. Discuss whether "in all things, charity" means acceptance and kindness in all matters or whether there are limitations to love. If so, what are those limits?

2. Do you think United Methodism has been too tolerant of theological and other types of diversity, or has it been too restricted in its understanding of grace? Or both?

3. United Methodists experience controversy on issues such as abortion and homosexuality. In these and other "hot button" issues, how do you see justice and love in harmony or conflict?

4. In what ways would you like to see the church demonstrate "in all things, charity"?

5

What Treasures United Methodism Should Conserve
Ruediger R. Minor

In my possession is a drawing that depicts three women. It is a picture of my wife, my mother, and my sister, drawn by our daughter at the age of three. It is one of the treasures that I hope not to lose. Why? As a proud parent I could claim that it already shows the future artist-to-be. However, I am not sure that many people will agree. It is a very personal matter, what we are keeping as a treasure. Its real value is determined by our heart; we cannot buy it, and it is certainly not for sale. For many years this drawing was on display on a wall in our apartment. When we recently went through our papers, we came across this picture and deeply enjoyed it.

When I think of United Methodist treasures, matters come to my mind that are not necessarily in the forefront of either the theological or the social or political debate; matters that we all may not even hold in common, but which in a distinctive way are close to our hearts.

Unity, Not Uniformity

Treasures are not consensus documents. I was reared in European Methodism, which in some ways differs and is distinct from Methodism in the United States. Therefore, some of the matters that I will refer to as "treasures" in this essay might not be of great value to some readers. When I met United Methodists in the United States, I learned to treasure new things. For example, I grew up with worship services that were plain in style and usually held in modest chapels. For a long time I thought this was "the" United

Methodist worship. Coming to the United States, I fell in love with a more ornate worship that expresses joy and reverence not only in words but also in a visible and dramatic form.

The Bible speaks of the "varieties" in the church (1 Cor. 12:4), signifying the manifold God-given gifts and graces. To celebrate our diversity as United Methodists does not contradict our strong sense of unity. Uniform stones would never form a magnificent mosaic. Methodism as a "connectional" church expresses this treasure of persons who accept each other in their diversity because they are held together in one spirit. In the same spirit we can also accept Christians of other denominations as our brothers and sisters and yet treasure the distinctive marks of Methodism. In his fine treatise on "Catholic Spirit," John Wesley reminds us that an ecumenical openness for others is based on the love and appreciation for one's own principles, but the heart builds the connection. He opens with the words of 2 Kings 10:15: "Is your heart right with my heart . . . give me your hand."

The Heart Matters

The heart recognizes the real treasures. John Wesley felt his heart "strangely warmed" when he experienced God's pardoning grace through faith at Aldersgate on May 24, 1738. He left us the legacy that faith matters are heart matters. Methodism witnesses to the personal structure of the Christian faith.

In my assignment to Russia, I found an interesting situation. Even former Communists in Russia speak about their "faith." It is understood as a system of beliefs and convictions that could easily be replaced by a new set; for example, nationalist-orthodox. In the same way some people understand faith as a set of emotions and feelings hardly to be distinguished from other psychic phenomena. Methodist witness holds the conviction that there is no "generic faith" (to borrow a phrase from George Morris), but Christian faith means a personal encounter with Jesus Christ.

This story is only one among many. A young man, a high school student from Russia, drops into the Methodist church in Tallinn. His appearance—green hair and worn-out jeans—is meant to

116

shock people, and normally it works. He is full of protest against his school and the Communist system. But there in the church people are not shocked. What is more, they invite him to take a seat, and for the first time in his life he hears a message he finds no reason to protest against. Later he confessed, "This hour changed my life." Christ has encountered him.

God Accepts Us for Christ's Sake

As United Methodists we share this personal understanding of faith with the other churches of the Reformation. The same is true for another treasure: the biblical understanding of justification by grace through faith. United Methodist Bishop Walter Klaiber from Germany challenged the European Lutheran and Reformed churches at an Ecumenical meeting in Vienna in 1994 to the continuing task of preaching justification by faith. He emphasized that justification by works has left the religious sphere to claim the practical-ethical sphere in the so-called "work ethic," especially in Protestantism.

Alluding to the language of the Reformers, I would define justification by works in such a way that persons do not qualify their work, but rather that persons are qualified by their work. The parameters are given by work and possession, but not by the person.

There is a lot of justification by works in our world today. This is not to denounce the value of disciplined work. However, the demise of Communism has lured many people into the naive belief that "rolling up our sleeves and hard work" could save the world and solve its manifold problems. What is even more serious, those who are less lucky and in disabling conditions succumb in a society that evaluates people only by their work and its result, the paycheck. That we "for God's sake" have worth as human beings outside our work and deeds—this would be a brief description of justification by faith. This is a very important and liberating message, a treasure worth keeping.

A Vital Faith

To declare faith matters as heart matters does not confine the faith to the inner life of a person. Methodists have always been living under the expectation to show their faith. This is true for its acquisition as well as for its expression.

While asserting that the Bible is the only source and true fountain for the faith (this again together with the other churches of the Reformation), United Methodists have valued reason, experience, and tradition as helpful in interpreting means for the formation of personal faith. Although in recent discussions this has sometimes been misinterpreted as if the Bible was just one among four sources of almost equal value, we should maintain the importance of this fourfold (quadrilateral) approach.

United Methodism has never been a fundamentalist, "Bible only" movement. The history of the faith, the common pilgrimage of the people of God, has always been an important witness and resource for the expression of our contemporary faith. Faith has conquered the world in the lives of Christian persons and communities. As we listen to their stories we get new insights into the victories and failures of our own pilgrimage. And in a time of a rising level of education that is, however, accompanied by an alarming growth of irrationalism, it is important to show that vital faith is a "reasonable" matter. United Methodism has a legacy to share that was appropriately expressed by a young Russian woman: "We Russians are an educated people. We learned to use our brains. In the Methodist church we can use our brains in dealing with the Bible, in expressing our faith."

A vital faith finds its expression in the community of believers, the church. The worshiping and serving community is close to the very heart of United Methodism. And in worship the congregation is not merely an audience; it is actively involved.

One classic expression of this involvement is congregational singing. United Methodism has a great treasure in its hymns, especially those written by Charles Wesley. Early Methodist hymnology reflects and shapes the life and faith of the "people called Methodists." It has been said that the whole doctrine and praxis of Methodism could be reconstructed from its early hymns, should all other documents be lost.

United Methodism has been open to contemporary expressions of the faith in worship and music. The rise of contemporary forms of worship and the readiness to accept them is a question of age and taste. But United Methodists must never forget their hymns lest they forfeit a great gift of God.

Servants for Jesus' Sake

Communal expression of the faith is not found only in worship. Consider the common farewell line in many United Methodist churches at the end of congregational worship: "The worship is over, the service begins." United Methodists have always looked upon the world as their parish. The world is the place to share the faith, and United Methodism has never been without the opportunity to be in mission.

However, one may ask whether United Methodism in its traditional strongholds in America and Europe has allowed this treasure to go to Africa and Asia. We should be careful not to connect too quickly the sharing of the gospel in mission and evangelism with numerical growth. United Methodism has remained a relatively small movement in most of the European countries but has contributed quite substantially to spiritual renewal in many places. Its principle has been to help persons find a vital faith in Christ, a challenge to share it, and a spiritual home.

One of the strengths of genuine Methodist evangelism was that our spiritual ancestors could discern between the call to accept Christ and the invitation into the membership of the Methodist Church. They did not recruit members for a spiritualized noninstitutional "church invisible." In our times of attention to denominationalism and confessionalism, we would be noble to remind ourselves and others that evangelism is aiming higher than our institutions. Our ancestors called it the kingdom of God. We may talk with modesty but no less endeavor about the servant-discipleship of the servant-Lord "that the world may believe."

Servanthood is the best description for the relationship of Methodism to the world. Although the Methodist movement has touched a substantial number of people in some countries, it was never tempted to provide the dominant form of religion. (The only exception might be Fiji; however, the tension there in recent years should sustain our caution.) And there are examples of United Methodist churches that, though representing only a fraction of the population, have been influential in their nations. (It would be interesting to look up the story of Methodism in Japan or Scandinavia or Austria.) United Methodism at its best proclaims Jesus Christ as the Servant-Lord and is striving to be conformed to his image.

All over the world conservative movements attempt to put a religious yoke on societies. This is true for non-Christian religions, but also for the resurgence of national churches in central and eastern Europe, as well as some forces of the "religious right" in the United States. However, the task for the church is not to turn the society into a new "Christendom," into a new church-led body, but to assist it in becoming a human and humanizing society. If we believe that to be a Christian is to become more human in a deeper sense, then the church should have an enabling influence in the world. And there is no better means for this influence than the gospel message of the saving and liberating Christ and a readiness to respond to the changes that are wrought by this gospel.

One of the most exciting ministries of The United Methodist Church in Russia is the prison ministry in Yekaterinburg. This ministry began with worship services held in the large hall for cultural events. In the meantime the prison administration has recognized the importance of this ministry and donated a classroom in an educational building. It was redecorated as a chapel by the prisoners. There are more than 2,000 men in this prison. It is moving to see them march to the worship hall, but it is even more moving to meet with the small group that comes to the chapel regularly. They come for Bible study and sharing. The chapel has become their hope center. This is clearly expressed in a painting on one of the walls: iron prison bars, but behind them a rainbow, the sign of hope in God's covenant. Even the correction officers feel the change of the prisoners. "You have softened their hard hearts," they tell our United Methodist people who work in this ministry.

The goal of the new Russian prison administration—to make the prison system more human—is important indeed if we think of the hardships of the Soviet prisons and "gulags." Because of the results of the prison ministry, the officers in the Yekaterinburg prison turned to The United Methodist Church for assistance in finding a new approach. With the help of United Methodist experts from the United States, a re-training course has been started to instruct the officers in psychology, conflict management, and other skills that have been developed in prison systems. The preaching of the gospel has created a desire in these people that is contributing to new patterns in a community. And the church is working as a catalyst. The United Methodist Mission Statement states our goal in mission: "transformed persons in a transformed society."

A Treasure in Earthen Vessels

One final caveat needs to be mentioned in our attempt to recount United Methodist treasures. This whole endeavor could be very foolish if we would use it *ad majored gloriam* (for the augmentation of glory) of The United Methodist Church. It would be easy to confirm in each of the above mentioned cases how Methodists did not keep their treasures but gambled them away. But it does not devaluate those treasures that they are sometimes hidden in mean-looking human structures.

"We have this treasure in earthen vessels, to show that the transcendent power belongs to God and not to us" (2 Cor. 4:7 RSV). It is sometimes through the "cracks" in those vessels, through our weaknesses and failures, that the glory of God shines brightly. For the real treasures of the church are not our virtues, traditions, and good deeds, but the "most-holy gospel of our Lord Jesus Christ."[1]

NOTE

1. A postscript in place of acknowledgments: This article was prepared and written literally on the road in episcopal service—in hotel rooms, railroad cars, and aircraft. I apologize for borrowing and using the ideas of many people, colleagues and good friends, without being able to give proper acknowledgment. I hope they will take it as a sign of my indebtedness to them in recognizing the treasures that God has bestowed on this United Methodist Church.

What Treasures United Methodism Should Conserve
S. Michael Hahm

Henry and Ella Appenzeller possessed a frontier spirit for mission, sharing the good news with the people of Korea, the Land of the Morning Calm. They were challenged to share the gospel of Jesus Christ with a people whose tradition and culture were unfamiliar to them. On Easter Sunday, 1885, Henry and Ella Appenzeller stepped onto the bare rocks of the Korean shore at Inchon in a cold drizzly rain. Ella later wrote that her husband, sensing the historical significance of the moment, knelt and prayed, "May he who this day burst the bars of the tomb bring light and liberty to Korea."[1]

A Frontier Methodist Church in Pyongyang, North Korea

I grew up in a local Methodist church about ten miles from Pyongyang, North Korea. From the moment the church was organized, it began to challenge the accustomed way of thinking, living, and believing. The Christian gospel began to affect all aspects of traditional ways of life and beliefs, which were deeply rooted in the Confucius and Buddhist traditions and teachings. Children received full attention and became nurtured in Christian teachings through worship and Sunday schools. Both men and women participated in the Methodist class sessions to learn about basic Christian beliefs. As they began to encounter the Bible, they not only learned how to read and write, but their eyes were opened to see who they were from a new perspective.

122

Through this small frontier local Methodist church, the congregation was challenged to proclaim the gospel of Jesus Christ so that people came to believe in him as Lord and Savior. They were challenged to confront sin and evil with prophetic courage and vision and to name the demons that held power over people and nations. The church began to participate in the people's struggles for dignity, freedom, and self-determination. Its mission challenge was clearly defined:

- to be in solidarity with the poor and to share with them;
- to be especially sensitive to the needs of those most vulnerable and marginalized;
- to support and nurture the children and youth in their church and community;
- to support equal rights for women; and
- to gather the community of faith and build up the Body of Christ.

These treasures United Methodism should continue to conserve.

Wesley's Teaching on God's Presence in the World

The frontier spirit of mission which drove the Appenzellers to Korea was prompted by John Wesley's admonition on God's presence in the world. They were following the Great Commission mandate of Jesus, who said, "All authority in heaven and on earth has been given to me. Go therefore and make disciples of all nations, baptizing them in the name of the Father and of the Son and of the Holy Spirit" (Matt. 28:18-19).

Eighteenth-century England saw many contrasts between the nobility and the poor. As the Industrial Revolution swept across England, masses of people were crowded into the industrial centers. However, they lacked minimal provisions for health, recreation, and education. At that time, the Church of England attempted to minister only to the spiritual and moral needs of these masses of people and, to a lesser degree, to their intellectual and social needs.[2]

While Wesley organized societies primarily for spiritual discipline and growth of the people, he also sought to serve the needs of the people, most of all, by taking the gospel to the people where they lived. The Wesleyan movement attempted to be in solidarity with the poor in order to transform their condition of marginalization. Furthermore, it tried to hear the cry of the poor and to enable the poor to become agents of change. Theodore W. Jennings claims that Wesley attempted to demystify wealth and power—what contemporary theologians call a "preferential option for the poor."[3]

For Wesley, there was no separation between holiness and worldliness. Thus spiritual holiness was grounded in active engagement with the world. To Wesley, stewardship was the practice of the agents of a new creation who gave "creation back to the Creator."[4]

Theologian John Cobb describes Wesley's theology in terms of God's presence in the world.[5] God is present in all persons as well as in the world. In the tradition of John Wesley, we United Methodists are called to reach out to all people throughout the world. We United Methodists must recapture the frontier spirit of mission touching all human lives and bringing the gospel of Jesus Christ to people on every continent, just as early American Methodist circuit riders went with the people to the frontier towns. This frontier spirit is a great treasure that we as United Methodists should conserve.

Biblical Mandates for Mission

In light of the central place of the frontier spirit of mission in the Wesleyan movement, United Methodists need to conserve and embody three biblical mission mandates for our present moment. First, we are called to proclaim the Jubilee declaration to all people for freedom and liberation from sin and oppression. Second, we are called to proclaim the Jubilee declaration for rectification of injustices. Finally, we are called to proclaim the Jubilee declaration for the vision of a new heaven and a new earth.

As explained in Leviticus 25, the fiftieth year following seven cycles of seven sabbath years (forty-nine years) is called a *jobel* or jubilee year. Jubilee is a time when "liberty" was proclaimed "throughout the land to all its inhabitants. It shall be a jubilee for you: you shall return, every one of you, to your property and every one of you to your family" (Lev. 25:10). The main focus is placed on the restitution of the original distribution of land property for all families.

In this prophetic tradition, Jesus announces "the year of the Lord's favor," Isaiah's eschatological promise (Luke 4:18-19). Jesus brings the kingdom of God through the prophetic proclamation of the Jubilee year: "the year of the Lord's favor." Jesus announces the kingdom of God with a specific Jubilee agenda which defines Jesus' own ministry.

For the first time since 1945, Christian representatives from North and South Korea met in Glion, Switzerland, in 1988. They proclaimed the year 1995 as the Jubilee Year of Korea. The intent of the proclamation was to enhance the Korean reconciliation process. Since this declaration, the biblical motif of Jubilee has gained increasing worldwide prominence.

How do we interpret Jesus' proclamation of "the year of the Lord's favor" in today's context? Was Jesus literally ushering in the Jubilee year, or just professing a utopian dream? Or was he spiritualizing or generalizing the meaning of the Jubilee?

I interpret Jesus' Jubilee proclamation as understanding Jubilee as God's concrete act of liberating humanity in the reign of God. The Jubilee year proclaims forgiveness of sins as well as liberation from the concrete political, economic, and social oppression.

Proclaiming Freedom and Liberation

In the year of Jubilee, freedom and liberation are to be proclaimed. Isaiah declares, "The LORD . . . has sent me . . . to proclaim liberty to the captives" (Isa. 61:1b). Jesus reiterated this passage in the synagogue when he spoke of freedom and liberation, and declared: "Today this scripture has been fulfilled in your hearing" (Luke 4:21).

In Jesus Christ people are free from sin and even death. Thus, Jubilee is not only a liberation from concrete forms of oppression, but also a freedom from the ultimate root of oppression, the inner bondage of sin. Christian freedom is part and parcel of the new order inaugurated by God in Jesus Christ.

Recently we have witnessed freedom movements throughout the world. The Berlin Wall came tumbling down. In South Africa the apartheid system was toppled. The wall of hostility between the Israelis and the Palestinians has finally begun to show cracks. At the present time, Korea may be the only country that still remains divided as a result of international decisions at the end of World War II. Yet there are people around the world enmeshed in political, ethnic, and tribal conflicts who are waiting for freedom and liberation. We as United Methodists have a strong heritage of liberating people out of their oppression and bondage.

United Methodists need to conserve a liberating understanding of Jesus Christ. Korean poet Kim Chi-Ha, in the drama "The Gold-Crowned Jesus" portrays a cement statue of Jesus outside an ornate cathedral.[6] Hungry beggars lie at its base. One cold wintry day, when they seek alms from a priest and a rich person, they are refused with contempt. Police are called to disperse the beggars. One pauper begins to cry, lamenting: "This Jesus might well be a savior to those who have enough to eat, who have a home and a family. But what has he to do with a beggar like me?" Suddenly he discovers with amazement that the statue of Jesus is crying, too. As he rips the gold crown from Jesus' head, he hears the statue speaking: "Take it, please! For too long time have I been imprisoned in this cement. . . . I wish to talk with poor people like you and share your suffering."

Jesus encourages the sale of the gold crown; a crown of thorns is sufficient. But then a policeman reappears with the priest and rich person. They snatch the gold crown and replace it on the cement Jesus. The beggar is dragged off to jail, and Jesus becomes once again entombed, silent, and petrified in stone.

If people only view Jesus Christ in gold-crowned statues or in stained-glass windows of the great cathedrals, he remains entombed. If, however, we introduce Jesus to the poor and the wretched of the earth, we liberate Jesus as a living Savior for millions of people who have been marginalized by the church and world. Truly,

126

We are called to the border to follow the One who crosses all boundary lines and tears down all barriers. Jesus was a Jew who dared befriend Samaritans, a carpenter who did not hesitate to challenge scholars, a male who was sensitive to women's experience, an activist who prayed continually, a Nazarene who confronted the power structure in Jerusalem. Jesus showed special concern for the poor and the marginalized, yet knew how to speak to the powerful. He stood rooted in the past while giving birth to a new heaven and a new earth.[7]

In the past, missionary enterprises often seemed to disregard or even annihilate indigenous cultures, carried out in alliance with military and colonialist powers. In the Americas the Spanish Christian conquerors destroyed advanced and colorful indigenous cultures for five centuries. In recent decades, many have drawn ties between mission and evangelism and the economic and technological domination of the world by Western powers.[8] In recent missionary movements, however, there has been a growing sensitivity to issues related to indigenous cultures.

Another important issue is how United Methodists understand the gospel in relation to women in the church and society. Cultural patterns of discrimination and oppression of women are rampant in many cultures. A global missional priority today is confronting these oppressive cultural patterns. An urgent need exists for greater justice for women in both church and society.

Proclaiming the Rectification of Injustice

In the second place, from the Jubilee perspective, our mission is to proclaim the rectification ("correcting" or "setting right") of things as they are, to announce the year of God's restoration, which is literally the meaning of the Jubilee and Atonement. Human sin produces social inequalities and the accumulation of power and wealth. Society needs periodic restructuring. In the words of Mary, God brings down the mighty and lifts up the lowly (see Luke 1:52). God promises rectification for people, especially those who are poor and oppressed. God in Christ comes proclaiming a kingdom of reversal, where the last will be first and the first will be last. God will usher in the new order, a new transformation, and demands repentance: "The time is fulfilled, the kingdom of God has come near; repent, and believe in the good news" (Mark 1:15). Jesus demands repentance from personal, social, and national sins.

In his book *A Conspiracy of Goodness,* Donald E. Messer introduces an image of the church and ministry as a community of fence movers.[9] Immediately after World War I, Quakers began to distribute food and clothing for the impoverished people of Poland. One relief worker suddenly contracted typhus and died within twenty-four hours. The village had only Roman Catholic cemeteries, and canonical laws forbade burying any non-Catholics in consecrated ground. The Quaker relief worker was buried in a grave just outside the cemetery. The next morning, however, the relief worker's grave was found inside the cemetery, for the villagers had moved the fence during the night. For Messer, the story of Polish fence movers embodies an enacted parable for our time. Polish Catholics defied outdated dogmas and practices which prevented the doing of justice.

Fence movers, in the spirit of Jubilee, challenge the seemingly permanent order. No system, no structure, no ideology is sacred. Until we reach the final Jubilee of the kingdom in its consummation, the rectification of the new order goes on. No society can go on indefinitely without a correction. Nor can the church remain unchanged. Rectification, however, is not complete without restoration. Jubilee proclaims renewal: the restoration of the people, of social relationships, and of nature itself.

A rich man asked Jesus how he could inherit eternal life. Since the man had always been faithful to the commandments, Jesus responded: "You lack one thing; go, sell what you own, and give the money to the poor, and you will have treasure in heaven; then come, follow me" (Mark 10:21). Shocked, the man refused to become a disciple. In the reign of God, the rich and powerful are asked to give up their wealth and power so that the poor and oppressed can be rectified, empowered, and restored.

In contrast, Zacchaeus, the tax collector, amends his life, saying to Jesus, "Look, half of my possessions, Lord, I will give to the poor; and if I have defrauded anyone of anything, I will pay back four times as much" (Luke 19:8). Because of his act of rectification and restoration, salvation comes to him and his house.

Jubilee, as the renunciation of power by the powerful, finds its fulfillment in the self-emptying power of Jesus Christ (see Phil. 2:6-8). The Jubilee message is not an aggressive grasping of power but humanity, brokenness, vulnerability, even death on a cross. Christ's self-emptying takes place so that others may be empowered—Samaritans, women, outcasts, oppressed political minorities, persons with disabilities, and many others.

Proclaiming a Vision of a New Heaven and a New Earth

Finally, from the Jubilee perspective our mission is to inaugurate the new age of the Lord. The church participates in the task of the in-breaking of the kingdom and celebrates in anticipation of its final consummation. We experience the kingdom of God now, but we also hope in the final coming of the kingdom. The Holy Spirit empowers us to transform the world to God's love. For this task we must struggle and suffer vicariously for the kingdom.

In our world today millions of people are waiting to hear of the vision of a new heaven and a new earth. Many Russians are experiencing tremendous difficulty in adjusting to a new uncertain political and economic world. Some in Moscow have committed suicide by jumping into the subway tracks.

Messer also describes the church as "a company of star throwers."[10] This image of mission is based on Loren Eisely's story of meeting a man who throws starfish into the breaking surf. Against great odds, he strives to preserve life. The United Methodist Church needs a multitude of star throwers, saving the lives of all of God's creatures. The church is called to be the community of star throwers, restoring life in the midst of death.

There are some ten million separated family members in Korea. Since the division of Korea five decades ago, these ten million people have not known whether their loved ones are dead or alive. What a tragedy that millions of people do not know whether their loved ones are still living or dead! A mother separated from her son tells the following story:

In my dream you have finally returned home. At the age of 14 you left hastily home, and after some forty years you finally returned to me. I have been hoping and praying for your return while I am still alive. I have been worrying about you day and night. . . . Finally you have returned home. You came and without saying a word you placed your head on my lap; you sobbed and sobbed uncontrollably for a long time. You cried like a child. You looked so pale, only skin and bones. . . . And then, finally, you said to me with tearful eyes, "I shall never leave you again, I shall never leave you again."

(unknown source)

Add to this mother and son the thousands of separated families around the world, the children in refugee camps without a sense of hope, the Moscow suicide victims, and the children in the forced labor camps, for whom we need to proclaim the Jubilee message of a vision of a new heaven and a new earth:

> For you shall go out in joy,
>   and be led back in peace;
> the mountains and the hills before you
>   shall burst into song,
>   and all the trees of the field shall clap their hands.
> Instead of the thorn shall come up the cypress;
>   instead of the brier shall come up the myrtle;
> and it shall be to the LORD for a memorial,
>   for an everlasting sign that shall not be cut off.

(Isa. 55:12-13)

What a Glorious Vision This Is!

When the people adhere to the Jubilee decree they will live in peace. They will enjoy the harvests they sow in their lands. They will live in the homes which they build. Old people will have vision for the future, and children will live a long life. When Jubilee comes, people will experience freedom from sin and death, and liberation from oppression. When Jubilee comes people will be rectified and restored to their sense of dignity, freedom, and self-determination as God's children.

Conclusion

In the tradition of John Wesley, Henry and Ella Appenzeller, and many others who were frontier persons in mission, United Methodists must conserve for the twenty-first century this global mission emphasis as one of its greatest treasures. We, too, must offer God's grace for salvation to all the world.

God is still challenging us to go into new frontiers of mission, sharing the good news for freedom and liberty from sin and oppression, to rectify injustices and restore God's reign, and to proclaim the vision of a new heaven and a new earth.

NOTES

1. See the *Christian Advocate,* Feb. 25, 1885, and Appenzeller correspondence.

2. Rupert E. Davies, *Methodism* (London: Epworth Press, 1985), pp. 22-23.

3. Theodore W. Jennings, *Good News to the Poor: John Wesley's Evangelical Economics* (Nashville: Abingdon Press, 1990), p. 21.

4. Ibid., p. 154.

5. John B. Cobb, *Grace and Responsibility: A Wesleyan Theology for Today* (Nashville: Abingdon Press, 1995), p. 41.

6. Chi-Ha Kim, *The Gold-Crowned Jesus and Other Writings* (Maryknoll, N.Y.: Orbis Books, 1978).

7. *International Review of Mission,* the San Antonio WCC Conference, vol. 78, nos. 311/312 (July/October 1989), p. 457.

8. Eugene L. Stockwell, "Mission Issues for Today and Tomorrow," the *San Antonio Report: Your Will Be Done, Mission in Christ's Way,* Frederick R. Wilson, ed. (Geneva: WCC Publications, 1990), pp. 122-24.

9. Donald E. Messer, *A Conspiracy of Goodness: Contemporary Images of Christian Mission* (Nashville: Abingdon Press, 1992), pp. 127-44.

10. Ibid., pp. 109-26. See Loren Eiseley, *The Star Thrower,* Kenneth Heuer, ed. (San Diego: Harcourt Brace Jovanovich, 1978), p. 172.

STUDY GUIDE

Two writers share their perspectives on what theological and ecclesiastical treasures United Methodism should conserve as it moves into the next century. Both express concern that the church retain its emphasis on mission. Reflecting from European and Korean experiences, they invite readers to cherish their own unique traditions as well as to embrace the church's diversity.

Ruediger R. Minor emphasizes the connectional nature of United Methodism, the evangelical spirit of a "heart strangely warmed," preaching justification by faith, the "quadrilateral" approach to theology, hymn singing, and an emphasis on being servants for Jesus' sake in the world.

S. Michael Hahm focuses on United Methodism's heritage of social justice and action around the globe. He underscores the Wesleyan commitment to the poor and the oppressed, and advocates retaining a frontier spirit of mission that seeks liberation and freedom for all peoples. He treasures United Methodism in mission offering a new vision of heaven and earth.

Items for Reflection

1. If you were to itemize the treasures of United Methodism you would want to conserve, what would you list?

2. What treasures (commitments or programs) do you fear the church has lost or may abandon in the future?

3. Both authors emphasized the imperative of mission to the life of the church. From your perspective, how high would you prioritize mission outreach among the treasures of United Methodism?

4. Evangelism and church growth are not excluded but certainly not emphasized in these essays. How do you feel about the status of both in contemporary United Methodism?

6

How United Methodism Must Change

Marjorie Hewitt Suchocki

When I first read John Wesley's *A Plain Account of Christian Perfection,* I was astonished at the implicit joy of the book.[1] God created us in order that we might live lives of love to the very fullest of our powers. To live in such a manner is to glorify God, for it fulfills God's will for creation. Our whole beings—intellect, will, affections, body—are to be developed to the fullest for this purpose. Furthermore, since God has created us toward this end, this is precisely the life that God makes available to us through Jesus Christ. Salvation is for the sake of sanctification.

The joy of the book is that by God's grace, a life of love is really possible! The endless yearning to be all that we can be for the sake of the deep richness of human community is no vain yearning, not ever to be denied hope. To the contrary, God calls us to a living hope, and empowers us for it. This is the life of Christian perfection: it is all of love, utilizing all our powers in its service. There is no holding back on the basis of gender or class or race. In Christ we are made free precisely so that we might become most fully ourselves in the service of God, which is at the same time a love of neighbor, a right regard for our own selves. By so doing, we glorify God.

Such a doctrine seemed to me then and since quite wonderful. It seems to me to be the essence of Methodism, for I know of no other tradition that so sings the life God makes possible for us together as a community of persons in Christ. Its hopefulness, confidence, and joy pervade the Wesleyan spirit. This raises the hope that as we inevitably encounter the challenges of change in

133

our time, we shall do so in the strength of this reappropriated Wesleyan doctrine.

Just as Wesley concludes *A Plain Account of Christian Perfection* with some remarkable "advices" to Methodists, I make bold to follow his lead by suggesting "advices" drawn from this book to guide us as we consider ways that United Methodists must change in our current climate of theological and cultural diversity. These "advices" concern prayer, pride, and perfection.

First, let us take seriously Wesley's admonition to be a continuously praying people. Second, let us learn humbly from Wesley's definition of pride as the unwillingness to learn from another. Third, let us open ourselves to "continue on to perfection."

On Becoming a Continuously Praying People

God does nothing but in answer to prayer; and even they who have been converted to God, without praying for it themselves (which is exceedingly rare), were not without the prayers of others. Every new victory which a soul gains is the effect of a new prayer. On every occasion of uneasiness we should retire to prayer, that we may give place to the grace and light of God, and then form our resolutions, without being in any pain about what success they may have. (p. 100)

Wesley's emphasis on the role of prayer in our communal life is remarkable. While exhortations to a life of prayer pervade the book, it is in the last pages that Wesley's words on prayer soar to amazing heights. Are we to take Wesley seriously on this matter? Is it the case that "God does nothing but in answer to prayer"? Surely God's work in the universe is quite independent of our praying! How can we take Wesley's words as anything other than hyperbole?

The context may explain the message, for Wesley is addressing God's work as it occurs among us humans. He seems to assume a cooperative work between us and God. It is as if God has indeed brought countless worlds into being, spinning the galaxies into space. But having created the universe, including our world, God now chooses to work *with* us in the world. Having brought creatures such as our small selves into existence, God's continuing acts of creation draw us into the work. There is an awesomeness to this grace—for how could we hope or dare to consider ourselves co-laborers with God? Clearly we ourselves have nothing to do with the sustenance of those distant galaxies! Nonetheless, in the smaller sphere of our own spaces, it is as if God delights to bring us into the work. This participation takes place as we answer God's invitation to prayer. Prayer is participation in God's love; thus it is also participation in God's works of love.

In *A Plain Account* Wesley particularly speaks about prayer in relation to God's work of converting and sanctifying grace. One might ordinarily think that conversion and sanctification are totally the work of God, independent of human participation, but not so for Wesley. Or rather, one might say that for Wesley these activities are totally the work of God in and through God's work with us. God invites us to use prayer to become partners with God in the deepest work of divine grace: salvation and sanctification. It is by grace that we are made partners in grace.

How is this possible? Wesley does not spell it out, other than to claim "God does nothing but in answer to prayer" (p. 100). But we can speculate that it is the unitive function of prayer that joins us to God's work—and indeed, that joins us to those for whom we pray. Prayer is the opening of ourselves to God's will. But God's will is boundless love, poured out for creation, inviting creation into itself. This love is not restricted—by definition it is boundless, since its source is the infinite God. Thus when we deign to pray for someone, we can be very sure that the one for whom we pray is loved by God. When we open ourselves to God's will for that person in prayer, we become joined to God's love. Perhaps it is as if God takes our own small love and joins it to God's own mighty stream of love toward the one for whom we pray. As we are tapped into God's love, our own love for the other grows, and we begin to mirror God's will for the person's well-being. Our actions then become conformed to our prayers, and we become instruments in God's hands, manifesting God's love. God pulls us into the divine work, in ways that often go beyond our knowing, in bringing about the results of prayer.

Prayer joins us not only to God, but to the one for whom we pray. Intercessory prayer weaves the other's needs into who we are. Wesley suggests this with his rather amazing instruction that we should confess the sins of others as our own: "We ought . . . to bear the defects of others and our own, to confess them to God in secret prayer" (p. 99). It is as if our intercessions for others join us to them, so that when we feel blockages within them to divine grace, we quietly name these before God not in judgment, but in contrition, as if they were our own. And in some cases it may indeed be that we are unwitting participants in their sin. Perhaps it is we ourselves who have created the circumstances within which these blockages occur. Attitudes of self-righteousness, or hostility, or condemnation toward the other—regardless of the "rightness" or "wrongness" of these feelings—can create a spirit of hindrance for the other, and cause the other to stumble. But regardless of our own direct participation, the very solidarity that we share in Christ is sufficient for our joining ourselves to those in whom we perceive "defects," quietly confessing our perceptions of their sins as well as our own. Wesley suggests that such prayers are received by God as an opening for converting and/or sanctifying grace in the ones for whom we so pray.

Finally, Wesley suggests that our own prayers are used by God in drawing both others and ourselves to lives of love, or holiness. "Although all the graces of God depend on [God's] mere bounty, yet is [God] pleased generally to attach them to the prayers, the instructions, and the holiness of those with whom we are" (p. 96). Prayer weaves us by God's grace into a genuine community of interwoven welfare, so that prayers affect the whole of what God can do with us and for us. The deep implication in all of Wesley's words on prayer in this small book is that intercessory prayer is participation in God's work of grace for God's people.

Jack Rogers, vice president of San Francisco Theological Seminary, tells me this story of the role of prayer in a national meeting of Presbyterians. The issues before the group were harsh, feelings were volatile, lines were drawn. There was much anxiety concerning the meeting, and so the planners did an unusual thing. Instead of arranging the first day of the meeting as a time to begin deliberations, they arranged that the first day should be spent entirely in prayer. And so the assembled folk gathered, and prayed for one another and for their joint work together for the full first day. And

136

to the grateful astonishment of all, when the group began to address its divisive issues on the following day, even though differences were clear, the animosity was gone!

Is this not an example of Wesley's admonition put to practice? "On every occasion of uneasiness we should retire to prayer that we may give place to the grace and light of God, and then form our resolutions, without being in any pain about what success they may have" (p. 100). Perhaps if we as United Methodists were open to God's love for one another by praying for one another—particularly for those with whom we most disagree—perhaps then we will "give place to the grace and light of God" in prayer. By doing so, we will be participating in God's own work.

And so my first advice concerning "how United Methodism must change" is simply that we must become more deeply a people of prayer. We must take seriously this aspect of Wesleyan holiness, interceding for one another, being drawn into God's own love for each other. In the joining created through such prayers, we might find that God can draw us each and all toward deeper communal holiness.

Pride: An Unwillingness to Learn from One Another

> Watch and pray continually against pride. . . . if you think you are so taught of God as no longer to need man's teaching, pride lieth at the door. Yes, you have need to be taught . . . not only by me . . . but by the weakest preacher in London; yea, by all. . . . To imagine that none can teach you but those who are themselves saved from sin is a very great and dangerous mistake. Give not place to it for a moment. (pp. 86-87)

We might ordinarily define pride in terms of thinking of ourselves more highly than we ought to think; it has been defined classically as an overreaching of one's allotted sphere. How remarkable is Wesley's definition of pride as being an unwillingness to learn from another! We might understand such a definition if it required that we learn from those we acknowledge as wise in the things of God, but Wesley will not allow it. Instead, he specifies an openness not only to those we consider weak in the faith, but even to those who do not share our Christian convictions. We are to learn even from those with whom we disagree!

How is this the antithesis of pride? The key is the implicit idolatry that lies in thinking we have nothing to learn from others. After all, as Wesley notes, none of us can "at all times apprehend clearly or judge truly" (p. 70). But consider the dilemma in which this places us. We believe only those things we consider correct— by definition, if we thought the thing were false, we would not believe it. But our minds are finite, "clogged," as Wesley puts it, and unable to reason clearly. We are in a circle, then: our imperfect minds are such that our knowledge is faulty, but we cannot know in which part the fault lies! Only God has perfect knowledge—ours is always partial, for "now we know in part."

Pride is the refusal to recognize our finite condition, and to arrogate to ourselves that which can only belong to God: perfect knowledge. Thus Wesley's definition of pride as the refusal to learn from another is in fact a variation on the ancient understanding of pride as thinking more highly of ourselves than we ought to think. Pride is the sin of idolatry, and its easiest entry into our lives is through our arrogant assumption that our own beliefs conform perfectly to the mind of God. Clearly, when we live and act from this assumption, there is no need to learn from another!

Wesley's definition of pride gives a new depth of importance to theological diversity within the church. When there is only one acceptable way of thinking about God and God's ways with us, we too easily slide into the idolatry of worshiping our thoughts of God, rather than God's own self. But when there is a diversity of ways to think, each can offer a spiritually healthy counter to the other, revealing the finitude of all our systems and inviting us to listen attentively to each other not to condemn, but to learn. Then theologies do their true work of pointing us beyond ourselves to the God who is more than we can think. Knowledge gives way to wisdom.

When we refuse to learn from others, we not only set up our own thinking as God's thinking, but in the process we block our path to holiness. Holiness, as Wesley says again and again, is "pure love, filling the heart and governing all the words and actions"

(p. 51). But the pride of idolatrous knowledge results in feelings of anger toward the other—often even of hostility toward the other, whose contradiction of ourselves defies the absolute identity of our thoughts with God's. How dare the other be so wrong, so opposed to the thoughts of God (by which, of course, we mean our own thoughts). Hostility easily becomes hatred, and the holiness of love that God graciously longs to give us is blocked. Thus Wesley advises those who seek holiness to beware of pride, which is to beware of thinking we have nothing to learn from another, even the "weakest preacher in all London" and those who do not share our form of faith.

If we are truly to own our Wesleyan heritage, and open ourselves to the merriment of trusting God to draw us into holiness, then there are surely strong implications for times when we experience strong diversity of opinions in the church. Wesley's words suggest that we actually listen attentively to our opponents to find where it is that they might have light that corrects our own faulty knowledge. Can we actually listen to each other deeply, not because we wish to prove the other wrong, but because of our own openness to God in and through the other? Who knows what learnings would come about were we truly to take to heart Wesley's injunctions against pride as we consider ways to deal with divergent opinions!

Wesley's injunctions to be open to learning from one another have profound implications for the continuing vitality of the church. Tradition, after all, is created in and through its own transformation. Every great thinker in the church's history was suspect in his (and occasionally her!) own time, for no great thinker ever merely repeated the past. Wesley himself is our best example, for he surely went beyond the Reformers, the medieval Scholastics, and the early church fathers in his unique interpretation of holiness. He was greatly attacked for the very doctrine that we now recognize as our richest and most unique heritage as Methodists. Wesley transformed the tradition, and was thus used of God in the continuous creation of the tradition! For the tradition is a becoming thing, marked again and again by its own God-guided transformation. Openness to others, even when those others speak words that seem dangerously "untraditional" to us, is also

139

our openness to God. But conversely, pride's refusal to listen to—much less learn from—the other can be a blocking of God's own work in the ongoing creation of the Christian tradition.

We are manifestly not God, and the "mind of Christ" we are beseeched to have refers not to knowledge of Christ, but to the love of Christ. Pride would change love to knowledge, and in the process, lose love. Wesley's "think and let think" position is precisely a counter to the idolatry of pride as the refusal to learn from another. The humility of owning our faulty intellectual abilities and being open to learning from one another is at the same time an opening of ourselves to God's gracious gift of growth in love, which is Christian perfection. Thus my second advice in these times of challenge and change is to let go of pride, and dare to listen and learn from each other.

Deal with Diversities in Spirit of Christian Perfection

Pure love, reigning alone in the heart and life, this is the whole of scriptural perfection. . . . [It is] an entire renewal in the love and image of God, so as to rejoice evermore, to pray without ceasing, and in everything to give thanks. (p. 52)

The "image of God" plays a strong role in Wesley's *Plain Account.* The phrase occurs again and again, for Wesley's doctrine of perfection is a conviction concerning the renewal of the image of God in our lives. This image, in turn, has two aspects: first, it is the restoration of the ability to love God in and through our neighbor, and second, it is a value of the fullest possible development of each person's unique potential. To reappropriate a Wesleyan doctrine of perfection, then, is to deepen our commitment to the social dimension of holiness that has been such a mark of Methodist people.

The key to both aspects of Wesley's use of the image of God is contained in his account of Adam. Structurally, the image of God relates to Adam's ability to use "to the glory of God, all the powers with which he was created. Since he was created free from any defect, either in understanding or affections, his body was then no

140

clog to the mind; it did not hinder his apprehending all things clearly, judging truly concerning them, and reasoning justly, if he reasoned at all. . . . Consequently, this law, proportioned to his original powers, required that he should always think, always speak, and always act precisely right, in every point whatever" (p. 69).

The point of this was not the perfection of obedience, but the perfection of love. Adam, presumably fully developed in all ways, should have been able to live fully into and from the love of God, such that this love formed his very being. This is the image of God, and it constitutes living to the glory of God. It glorifies God precisely because it mirrors, reflected freely in the created order.

But in the traditional story, Adam fell, and his original perfection was lost. Wesley considers this to have resulted in certain irreversible effects for Adam's progeny, the most important of which is the new fragility and corruptibility of the human body. This, in turn, interferes with our capacity for knowledge; it is why we should expect that we will always be in some form of error, because it is as natural for us "to make a mistake as to breathe" (p. 70).

Finally, under the conditions of corruptibility, it is no longer possible for us to live in the perfect obedience possible to Adam. The ability to live solely for and from the love of God is seriously impaired.

For Wesley this is the beginning of the story; surely not the end. The whole point of Christ is the correction of the fault, the removal of the blockage to God's will of love for creation. Christ perfectly fulfills all law, and thus frees up the way for the life of love that God intends for creation through us human creatures. Faith unites us to Christ, and in this union we become participants in the ability to glorify God through lives of love. The obstacles of corruptibility are not removed from us: Christ does not restore for us the possibility of absoluteness of knowledge in our finite condition. What Christ restores is that which knowledge was to serve: the love of God. In Christ, we are freed to love. This, for Wesley, is the renewal of the image of God in us.

The other aspect of the renewed image has to do with the responsibility to become all that we can be within the conditions of our finitude. We were created for the sake of the divine image, so that the fullest development of our whole selves should witness

141

to the glory of God in creation. To be freed in Christ, then, implies a deep value of human potentiality. Further, the fullest development of our potential is in order to place the whole of who we are in the service of God's love. The freedom in Christ is the fullest possible development of who we are and can be for the sake of living fully in, from, and for God's love.

Essentially, it matters not whether Adam is a historical figure or not; what is conveyed through the picture of Adam is not humanity as it was, but humanity as it might be when freed through the love of God for the love of God and neighbor. We are called, each of us, to the fullest development of our intellects and our affections, and this development is to be for the sake of and in the service of being as open as possible to the love of God. Under the conditions of a finite creation, there is not one single pathway of development for all, for as Wesley says, we are "hedged in by outward circumstances" (p. 50). To develop to the fullest is correlated to one's unique giftedness, and results in such diversity that the praise and love of God is not manifest in one monochromatic sameness, but in the many-colored richness of diversity, bound together in love. And this is Christian perfection.

Wesley defines Christian perfection again and again, deeply concerned by the charge leveled against the doctrine that it implied a uniform life of never making any mistakes at all. Perfection is not of intellect, not of bodily health, not of social or cultural definitions of "politeness." It does entail the fullest development of all our powers, to whatever degree the limitations of our finitude make possible. But this development is itself in the service of love, so that we might exercise love to the fullest of our capacities. Perfection is a "renewal of the heart in the whole image of God, the full likeness of [the One] that created it. . . . It is the loving God with all our heart, and our neighbor as ourselves" (p. 109).

That this definition of holiness undergirds the Methodist tradition of social and personal holiness is evident in the following passage.

> One of the principal rules of religion is, to lose no occasion of serving God. And since [God] is invisible to our eyes, we are to serve [God] in our neighbour: which [God] receives as if done to [God's own self] in person, standing visibly before us. (p. 103)

Perfection entails lovingly serving God in and through our neighbor. But who, goes the ancient question, is our neighbor?

Scripture suggests a twofold answer: the despised stranger, and also the Christian who is beside us. Luke 10 teaches us from the dual vantage point of the Samaritan and the injured man that the neighbor is the one we would least expect to help us. The neighbor is the one separated from us by boundaries of culture, tradition, privilege, and hatred. The neighbor is the one we are most reluctant to address as "neighbor": but in this one, we are called to love and serve God. Under this definition, "neighbor" is sadly easy to identify: the neighbor is gay, or lesbian, or poor, or racially defined, or liberal, or conservative, or whoever it is that we identify as the one most distant from ourselves.

John 14 supplements this by suggesting also a nearer neighbor. The setting is the eve of the crucifixion, and the disciples are portrayed as anxious—as well they ought to be! The one they so loved and revered was to be taken from them. Jesus responds to their fears by telling them that the Paraclete will come to be their comfort, their sustenance, their encouragement.

The actual meaning of Paraclete is "the helper who is alongside you." Jesus says there will be a Paraclete like himself with the disciples—concrete, touchable, alongside them. Yet we have come, rightly, to identify this Paraclete as the Holy Spirit. Does this not imply that the Holy Spirit is given to each disciple, the brother or sister in Christ, who is alongside us? The suggestion is that the Holy Spirit is given to us not for our own sake, but for the sake of our neighbor. When we look for the Spirit, we are to find that Spirit in our Christian neighbor. What a church we would have if we looked expectantly at every brother or sister as bearer of the Spirit for us!

Wesley's suggestion, coupled with the scriptural implications of "neighbor," suggest that God stands visibly before us, whether near or far. Christian perfection is expressed, then, in our love for our neighbor, whether near or far. And that love will take on the task of love, breaking the boundaries of hostility, seeking the binding of God's own Spirit.

My final advice is that we earnestly seek to be a people "continuing on to perfection," exercising all of our judgments and actions by the criterion of the love of God. As we judge the changes that challenge us, let us ask whether they promote the renewal of the image of God in us, in our congregation, in our wider communities. Do these changes promote the wonder of God present to us in our neighbor? Do they express a yearning for the fullest possible good of the neighbor? Do they look to the social conditions that make for the widest possible well-being? And when we find as a Christian community of United Methodists that we agree to the general goal, but disagree as to the specifics ("what, exactly, constitutes well-being?"), can we approach the heated debates with the awesome sense that in this one with whom we debate, God is present to and for us? If we can reappropriate Wesley's doctrine of holiness, the answers truly can be "yes." No wonder the doctrine inspires hope, and confidence, and joy!

If, then, we deal with our diversities in a spirit born of Wesley's understanding of Christian perfection, then we will intercede for one another in prayer. We will be open to learning from one another, and be cautious of idolatrously deifying our own opinions. We will yearn for full development of all persons' potentials, that their whole beings shall be available for the service of God in love. And we will learn to see God in our neighbor, both the neighbor who is near and the neighbor who is far.

Conclusion

How, then, should United Methodism change? We should become more deeply ourselves, drawing upon Wesley's insights concerning Christian perfection. In its dynamism, of course, we as the church will be continuously recreated by God's Spirit. In and through our praying, our learning from one another, and our loving one another, the Spirit moves, showing us what we may by God's grace yet become.

NOTE

1. John Wesley, *A Plain Account of Christian Perfection* (London: Epworth Press, 1952). All references in this essay are to this volume.

How United Methodism Must Change
Jerry L. Walls

One telling sign of institutional decline comes when an institution falls into a consistent pattern of majoring in minor points and minoring in major ones. When this occurs, we have the opposite of the ideal expressed in the slogan: "In essentials, unity; in non-essentials, liberty; and, in all things, charity." The United Methodist Church must change its emphases at the fundamental level in order to embody this ideal and reverse its pattern of decline.

Of Gnats and Camels

A memorable biblical version of the warning against minoring in majors and majoring in minors comes from our Lord himself. Speaking to the Pharisees of his day, he said: "You blind guides! You strain out a gnat but swallow a camel!" (Matt. 23:24). It is highly instructive to consider how this passage was recently cited by a leading bishop in response to the hundreds of letters he had received protesting United Methodist involvement in a much publicized conference at which basic Christian doctrines such as the Incarnation and Atonement were called into question and even ridiculed. The widespread alarm, according to the bishop, was unwarranted. Indeed, all the energy expended protesting the event was to the bishop an example of misguided United Methodists straining out gnats while swallowing camels. And what camels are we swallowing, in his judgment? He noted the problems of drug sales on the streets and the pervasive violence in our society.[1]

Now I would not characterize the bishop's concerns as gnats. To the contrary, they are extremely important. However, his response to the controversy shows that he clearly has things out of proportion. Those who take the gospel seriously should certainly be concerned about problems like drug abuse and violence. But the gospel itself is foundational to distinctively Christian engagement with such issues. And it was the distinctive content of the gospel itself that was under fire at the conference in question. Expression of deep concern when the very substance of the gospel is challenged from within the church should hardly be characterized as straining out gnats. Indeed, so far as *relative* importance is at issue, it appears the bishop has things exactly backward.

Let us consider now an area in which The United Methodist Church should allow liberty, but often does not. Perhaps there is no better example than the rigid insistence on "inclusive" language in many contexts. Seminary students and candidates for ordination are often pressured to avoid traditional pronouns for God and even discouraged from referring to him as Father, while references to human beings are scrutinized with a watchdog determination which matches or exceeds that of any right-wing zealot.

I would readily grant that a case can be made for "inclusive" language in reference to human beings, and I have no quarrel with those who prefer to use such language for theological or relational reasons. However, we are not allowing liberty in nonessentials if such linguistic conventions are insisted upon. Such language is, arguably, an implication of certain facets of the gospel. However, the use of such language does not rank with the Incarnation, the bodily resurrection of Jesus, or the forgiveness of sins through his death on the cross. Certainly, it has very little support from tradition, and even today the sensibilities of Christians vary widely on this matter.[2] To insist upon its use is surely to exemplify the "gnat-camel" syndrome.

The Importance of Truth

This brings us to a basic reorientation The United Methodist Church must undergo if it is to regain a sense of perspective and a proper focus on the gospel. What we profoundly need is a renewed conviction about the fundamental importance of truth and of our knowledge of it.

Merely to broach such a suggestion tends to make postmodern people uneasy. We are suspicious of any talk about truth, and we are doubly suspicious of any claim to know the truth. Such claims to truth are, we instinctively feel, dubiously motivated. Since no one really knows the truth, especially about highly controversial theological and ethical matters, anyone who claims to do so must be misguided and intent upon controlling others or manipulating them.

The United Methodist Church has guarded against these dangers for several decades with its policy of doctrinal pluralism. Such was the reality long before pluralism was officially affirmed as a principle in 1972. Of course, the present *Discipline* has retracted much of the earlier celebration of pluralism and reasserted the more classically orthodox position for our church. However, pluralism remains the reality at all levels of our church, including the Council of Bishops.

In many ways, doctrinal pluralism is the ecclesiastical counterpart to the more general cultural relativism which pervades Western society. As Allan Bloom argued several years ago in *The Closing of the American Mind,* the openness of cultural relativism has been transmuted into a mind-set that is, ironically, closed to the possibility of truth.[3] By contrast, the traditional virtue of openness was motivated by a desire to find the truth and a confidence that it could be discovered by reason.

Christian believers have even more reason to be humbly optimistic that we can know the truth than do traditional educators. For Christians are not left merely to their own resources in their efforts to find the truth. The Christian tradition claims to have revelation from God that tells us what he is like, what the purpose of life is, what is the right way to live, and so on. Without this conviction, believers forfeit what is distinctively Christian in their position.

Do We Believe in the Christian God?

The United Methodist Church must decide whether or not it believes God has revealed himself to us. If we believe he has, there is no evading the further claim that we know the essential truth

God intended to reveal. If we are unwilling to press this claim as well, the more general claim that God has revealed himself is merely formal and void of substantive content. Indeed, if we do not know the essential content of God's revelation, then the very claim that God has revealed himself is undermined.

Do we then know the essential content of what God revealed, and if so, can we identify it? These are the questions we must answer if we are to keep faith with the Christian tradition in its insistence that the gospel is God's word of salvation to the world. The Christian tradition, despite its differences and regrettable divisions, has maintained a striking consensus in returning a positive answer to these questions in its agreement that the ecumenical creeds express the essence of its faith. If we reject these creeds as faithful expressions of the substance of the faith, the inevitable result must be agnosticism about the meaning of Scripture, and even doubt whether it has an objective meaning at all. This is what we are witnessing today, and in such a context, the very claim that Scripture is revelation loses its force.

Suppose a group of high level executives paid a hefty fee to attend a seminar conducted by a communications expert who was reputed to be the "best in the business." After the day-long event they sit down to process it, and they discover that they cannot agree on what the speaker's main points were. They found the event stimulating, but they are not sure what the speaker meant to convey. In such a case, surely questions must be raised about the effectiveness of this communicator, not to mention the size of his fee!

Reflect now on the fact that God is supposed to be perfectly wise and perfectly good, as well as all powerful. It is such a God, the Christian tradition claims, who set out to reveal himself to people who were badly in need of light and salvation. He began this process by revealing himself initially to the nation of Israel over a period of many years. This revelation set the stage and prepared the way for his highest and ultimate revelation in Jesus of Nazareth.

Consider the implications of this. If God went to such great lengths to communicate with us, is it not most reasonable to believe the recipients of his revelation would grasp what he intended to convey? This is not to say that they would grasp it immediately. Indeed, the New Testament shows the disciples were slow to discern what Jesus was about. However, it is a denial of revelation to think they did not eventually understand what Jesus intended to teach them.

In the same vein, the classic creeds represent the church's best efforts to understand and articulate the scriptural account of who Jesus was and how God was revealed through him. If the consensus on matters of such central importance is wrong or mistaken, the claim that the church has revelation from God is undercut. Indeed, the idea of a revelation whose essential meaning was misconstrued by its recipients, and remains indeterminate, is a deeply incoherent notion. This is particularly evident if the alleged revealer is reputed to be as providential as the Christian God. Surely such a God could successfully communicate his message were he to choose to reveal himself.

This is the most fundamental issue we face as a church; namely, do we believe in the Christian God? Do we believe in a God who is personal, almighty, perfectly good, perfectly wise, who has existed eternally in three persons, the second of whom became incarnate in Jesus of Nazareth, died for our salvation, and was raised bodily from the dead? Notice that belief in such a God implies a strong view of revelation, and a strong view of revelation underwrites this conception of God. In other words, these beliefs are mutually supportive and confirming. Indeed, there is a sort of circularity here, but it is not the sort of vicious circularity in which we try to prove one belief by another only then to purport to prove the latter by assuming the former. Rather, we have here an example of a web of beliefs that are woven together in such a way that it is not clear which, if any, has epistemic priority, and thus, which would be proved by which. Clearly, however, God's trinitarian nature is the logically and ontologically more basic belief.

Belief in the Christian God is a robust belief that warrants a confident belief in his revelation and a correspondingly strong belief in the ecumenical creeds as summaries of the essential meaning of that revelation. On the other hand, a denial of any of these leads to the diminished gods of much contemporary theology, gods that are simply not worthy of belief.

149

Our Amorphous Identity

Happily, the theological statement of the current *Discipline* aligns The United Methodist Church with the doctrines of the creeds. Unhappily, what is official doctrine is not embraced with sufficient integrity across our church to give us a clear sense of theological identity and discipline.

The "Re-imagining" conference is only the most vivid reminder of this reality. A more profound gauge of our amorphous theological identity and lack of theological integrity is in the sort of responses from various leaders to the critics of the conference. Those who were critical of the conference, who argued that crucial doctrinal boundaries had been transgressed, who even dared to raise the specter of heresy, were themselves roundly criticized. We have witnessed the same sort of reaction to the recent Confessing Movement. Both the critics of Re-imagining and the advocates of Confessing have been characterized as zealots who brandish a highly personal and unduly narrow version of orthodoxy. For instance, a former member of the General Board of Church and Society recently warned United Methodists to "beware of a self-proclaimed Confessing Movement that seeks to redefine our Methodist heritage with a litmus test of 'adherence' to 'orthodoxy' as defined by the movement's members."[4]

The Truth Will Make Us Free

This characteristically modern-postmodern mind-set stands as a major obstacle to our willingness to embrace the truth. We do not see *truth as a reality,* which is liberating. We see only dubiously motivated *claims to truth,* which need to be guarded against because they lead to intolerance and abuse, claims that must be resisted and fended off.

It is a very telling sign of this mentality when a call for faithfulness to the heart of Christian doctrine, doctrine that is clearly contained in our own historic confessions, is characterized as an attempt to impose a personal litmus test. Matters of historic ecumenical consensus are reduced to one more special interest claim that has no more authority than any other personal opinion and must therefore be opposed in the name of liberty.

150

If we are to ever get beyond this mind-set, we must be captured again by what Pope John Paul II has called the "Splendor of Truth." We need to understand again that the truth makes us free and that our knowledge of it is essential to our fulfillment. Indeed, it is the denial of objective truth and the notion that all truth claims are thinly veiled personal agendas that opens the door to intolerance and abuse. If there is no objective truth that stands above our personal agendas, then all disputes are reduced to power struggles, and those with the most power have no good reason to refrain from imposing their will on the less powerful.[5]

Where Is the Unity?

Those who reject traditional doctrine as normative for all Christians must recognize that their position is just that: a position. It does not agree with the historic position of the church, but it is nevertheless a position. It is not a higher level negotiation that transcends positions that are more forthrightly exclusive. Rather, it is a denial of the view that essential unity involves agreement on historic Christian doctrine. Those who propose a different, allegedly higher, basis for unity must recognize that they are asking orthodox, evangelical believers to deny what they believe is essential.

If we cannot agree to reclaim our historic doctrinal heritage with full integrity, where does this leave us? I am afraid that it leaves us with a vague call for charity, which ignores a substantive basis for unity as well as distinct lines for liberty. Isn't love enough? Surely those who affirm historic Christianity as well as those who deny it but still adhere to at least selected portions of Jesus' moral teachings can agree to love each other, just as they believe they should love Jews, Muslims, Hindus, Buddhists, New Age proponents, secularists, atheists, racists, sexists, neo-pagans, and neo-Nazis. And presumably, many of these will return our love. But whether this is a sufficient ground of unity for a Christian church is another matter.

151

NOTES

1. United Methodist News Service press release, November 4, 1994.

2. A poll conducted a few years ago by the *United Methodist Reporter* found that 56.8 percent of its readers said they "much prefer to avoid" the use of "inclusive" language when referring to other people during worship, while another 12.8 percent said they were "mostly uncomfortable" with such language. See *United Methodist Reporter,* June 1, 1990.

3. Allan Bloom, *The Closing of the American Mind* (New York: Simon and Schuster, 1987), pp. 34, 38-40.

4. Martin Deppe, "Beware of a Self-Proclaiming Confessing Movement," *Christian Social Action,* September 1995, p. 32.

5. See Thomas A. Russman, *A Prospectus for the Triumph of Realism* (Macon, Ga.: Mercer University Press, 1987), pp. 93-107.

STUDY GUIDE

Addressing the issue of how United Methodism must change, both authors choose to speak primarily of theological issues, rather than questions regarding stances on social issues, reform of the itineracy, or structural revisions.

Marjorie Hewitt Suchocki recounts the teaching of John Wesley that emphasizes the power of prayer in overcoming divisions, the definition of pride as being unwilling to learn from others, and perfection of love meaning reaching out to our neighbor in need.

Jerry Walls focuses on recovering allegiance to the classical creeds of Christianity, deploring theological pluralism and emphasizing the truth of biblical revelation.

Items for Reflection

1. Do you feel that your pastor or church fails to teach and preach the classical doctrines of Christianity?

2. If you were to change United Methodism, what revisions would you emphasize?

3. Should inclusive language both in reference to God and humanity be stressed in the church?

4. Is Christian truth clearly expressed in the ancient creeds? Is God still revealing truth to us today? If there is revelation today, how is that revelation to be related to past revelation?

7

Unity and Disunity in United Methodism: A Way Ahead

William J. Abraham and Donald E. Messer

Whenever the late Albert Outler was introduced publicly to Free Methodists, he used to quip gleefully, "United Methodists are as united as Free Methodists are free." The cleverness of this remark derives from the way a sensitive subject is hedged about by ambiguity. The listener is left to fill in the material content, in this case the degree of unity or freedom posited. The beauty of a saying like this is that one can think the worst without having to say so openly and explicitly; indeed at the very same time one can say something witty or profound.

The phrase "in essentials, unity; in non-essentials, liberty; and, in all things, charity" has an equally pleasing ring about it. The listeners or readers find themselves drawn into an immediate commitment to unity, liberty, and charity, yet some of the most contested issues in the Christian tradition are at the same time left entirely unresolved. After all, the obvious questions here are (1) how exactly do we demarcate the essential from the nonessential, and (2) how do we articulate the deep meaning of liberty and charity? Yet we are drawn into a fruitful conversation in which everyone has a stake from the outset. We can even live with the fact that our slogan has not solved the deep problems of unity which it has so often been drawn on to address.

We want to do all we can do to foster a deep conversation between very different positions within our church. The more we have been involved in such dialogue, and the more we worked with the essays that make up this volume, the more convinced we became of the value of the discussion. Yet it would be foolish to hold that we do not face stormy waters ahead. Going under the ice can only be a temporary resting place of us all. Eventually we shall have to face whatever storms may emerge; the bridges we have sought to build may then prove crucial for the unity and general welfare of the church.

Many are afraid that our denomination shall come apart whether we like it or not. We are already deeply divided, they say; all that is needed is a trip wire to send us into schism. Others lament the very mention of schism, afraid that such talk will be a self-fulfilling prophecy. Better, they say, to muddle through and hope for the best. By now, however, we have already made mention of schism, so there is no going back. We need to face the prospects and do all in our power to deal with reality. It is a sign of a healthy tradition that it can name its problems and set about addressing them; it is a sign of a dysfunctional tradition that it refuses to identify its difficulties and deal resolutely with them. In this concluding epilogue we would like to give our suggestions as to further action and reflection.

Further Action and Reflection

1. We heartily commend conversation, formal and informal, around our chosen slogan. Our theme of unity, liberty, and charity gives us a meaty network of themes, which will stretch everybody who comes to the table. All we can do to foster mutual understanding and love is intrinsically worthwhile. Moreover, exchange of views breaks down flat stereotypes, opens up elements in our own position that we have not ourselves seen, and sends us home to think and pray.

2. A very heartening development is the extent to which lines of convergence begin to appear. Thus one of the wonderful surprises that emerged from our discussions was the extent to which "liberals" were intent on identifying material doctrines like sin, justification, and sanctification as crucial elements in the tradition. Equally, it is clear that "evangelicals" have not the slightest interest in abandoning the social dimensions of the faith like social justice, equity for all, and concern for the poor. Both sides are willing to work with and yet also examine critically the place of Scripture, tradition, reason, revelation, and experience in the

154

quest for intellectual light and integrity. Very often we are more right in what we affirm than in what we deny. It is extremely important that we work on identifying and naming areas of deep and substantial agreement. Such convergence is crucial in fostering respect, tolerance, and a fund of goodwill. We ought to sit down more often and name those deep convictions, teachings, practices, or doctrines to which we are all committed. In the process we also shall identify the marked differences that continue to exist in regard to both doctrine and social justice issues.

3. Clearly, all sides share a concern to proceed with the work of mission and witness. Some people see this work as so important that it sets the context in which they seek to identify the essentials of the tradition. Drawing on the past, listening carefully to the Holy Spirit, they seek to discern the call of God in the present. Others are more cautious about this posture, for they are wary of any move to allow the culture to set the agenda for the church. The church for them is first and foremost a divine society which has been given, through revelation, a clear mandate on its mission. Faithfulness to that mandate always takes precedence over relevance to culture. Either way, however, mission is a priority. In fact, there is an unspoken assumption that, whatever God wills for us in mission cannot be adequately discerned from the sidelines. Intellectual articulation and practical obedience go hand in hand in finding our pilgrim way into the future.

In light of this, we are convinced that United Methodism could make enormous progress if we could reach agreement on mission. Some are drawn to the making of disciples as the way ahead. Others fear that this strategy will be interpreted and implemented in narrow or even bureaucratic categories, ignoring the full force of the Great Commandment to love God and love the neighbor. They would prefer to work with Wesley's mandate to "reform the Nation, particularly the Church, and to spread scriptural holiness over the Land" as the core mission of the church. It would be unwise and premature to resolve this difference. However, it is hard to see how we could make disciples without so forming people in faith that they are equipped to reform the nation and church; and it is equally difficult to see how we can reform the nation and church without the making of genuine disciples. Indeed the hallmark of discipleship in our tradition is to make the kind of disciples who will spread scriptural holiness throughout the land. So there is room here for convergence and enrichment in articulating a common mission. With this in place the spotlight would then shift to nurturing each other in implementation and finding the deep doctrinal and intellectual resources needed to get the job done.

To be sure, reaching agreement on mission is itself a doctrinal decision. Here it is always possible to protest that we first need agreement in doctrine before we can proceed further. However, this is an incoherent claim, for agreement on mission is agreement in part in doctrine. We need to take this first step as best we can and then build from there to deeper levels of unity. This approach to convergence has deep roots in our tradition, and it is a psychologically wise way to proceed.

4. It is obvious that, however we proceed, there will be differences of opinion. We found that fascinating differences emerge even among those identified as "liberals" or "evangelicals." Properly articulated, these differences can evoke a healthy effort to bring out the best in our positions rather than simply lead to adverse criticism.

We can think of the internal traditions within our church as competing teams which bring out the best in each other's players by engaging them in a friendly contest. At times the followers of the various teams can take to brawling with each other after hotly disputed encounters. Yet leaders on both sides know that they can face their opponents with integrity and flair. "Evangelicals" clearly want to insist on the values of the past; "liberals" tend to stress the importance of contemporary relevance and credibility. Yet possibly "liberals" are often too quick to accept the values of the culture as binding; while "evangelicals" can be insensitive to the richer diversity of the tradition. And advocates on each side are too ready to close their eyes to the valuable insights of the other. There are few more apt ways to explore such strengths and weakness than by entering into extended conversation on topics of real substance. We clearly need faith and criticism; all sides bring their measure of both to the table.

5. We need to be very careful in identifying the ultimate outcome of our conversations. Premature closure is to be avoided like the plague. Yet it is good to dream dreams and see visions. It is clear that much of the consensus that has held us together over half a century is breaking down. Much of that consensus was procedural. We have invested a lot of energy in correct process, both administratively and doctrinally. We have been held together by leaders, many of whom were richly formed in the mainline theological developments of the twentieth century but who have not always known how to handle "evangelicals" other than by keeping them at the margins of the church. "Evangelicals," for their part, have often exploited the rhetoric of pluralism, all the while railing against its inadequacy as a working theology for the church. At times they have not known how to handle the alienation they have suffered and sometimes helped to create.

An Invitation to Work Toward Agreement

We now need to find and own a deep and rich consensus in faith. This is not a call to grow into some kind of muddled middle or to embrace a body of paper slogans or themes. It is an invitation to work out deep and lasting agreement in the essentials and nonessentials of our tradition, that our "hearts may be encouraged as they are knit together in love, to have all the riches of assured understanding and the knowledge of God's mystery, of Christ, in whom are hid all the treasures of wisdom and knowledge" (Col. 2:2-3 RSV).

Such a bold venture will take time and effort to construct together. It will require extensive listening to our own past history, for we cannot walk away from the past without becoming prisoners of our own time and space. It will also require careful attention to present voices, for we cannot ignore contemporary concerns and criticisms without becoming captives of a time gone by. It will demand extensive exchange from the whole range of opinion and conviction in the church, for it cannot be a power play by this or that group in the church. It will depend upon much struggle and prayer, for only the naive will think that such a consensus can be attained easily or from within our own resources. It will also

157

require a fresh outpouring of the Holy Spirit at every level of our life together, for in the end the church is the Body of Christ, led and empowered by the Spirit, to the glory of the Father.

Even so, come, Holy Spirit, come!

> come to us, and among us;
> come as the wind, and cleanse us;
> come as the fire, and burn;
> come as the dew, and refresh;
> convict, convert, and consecrate
> many hearts and lives
> to our great good
> and to thy greater glory;
> and this we ask for Jesus Christ's sake. Amen.[1]

NOTE

1. "An Invitation to the Holy Spirit," *The United Methodist Hymnal* (Nashville: The United Methodist Publishing House, 1989), p. 335.

STUDY GUIDE

Amid unity and disunity in United Methodism, the coeditors, William J. Abraham and Donald E. Messer, acknowledge that the "essentials/nonessentials" slogan does not solve the deeper issues of unity, liberty, and charity, though it draws us to deeper commitment to these Christian values.

A healthy denomination names its problems and sets about addressing them. Suggestions for further action and reflection include (1) continuing conversation around this theme, (2) identifying lines of theological and social justice convergence among "liberals" and "evangelicals," along with marked differences, (3) making mission and witness a priority of United Methodists, (4) criticizing forthrightly but fairly one another's perspectives and positions, and (5) avoiding premature closure and consensus while searching for unity.

The coeditors extend an invitation to both "evangelicals" and "liberals" to work out together a deep agreement regarding the essentials and nonessentials of United Methodism, listening to voices of both past and present, and drawing upon a fresh out-pouring of the Holy Spirit at every level of our life together.

Items for Reflection

1. Are the problems facing United Methodism so serious that schism is inevitable? Or are there ways problems can be identified and resolved?

2. List areas of convergence or consensus that unite Christians within our denomination. Specify also where marked differences continue to exist in regard to doctrine and social justice issues.

3. How would you define the core mission of the church? Can "evangelicals" and "liberal" find agreement on mission, even as they struggle to find agreement on doctrine and other issues?

4. During this study, depending on where you are on the continuum between "liberal" and "conservative," what have you learned positively from people who think theologically different from yourself?

5. What would you envision could happen to United Methodism, if we could overcome our polarization and politicalization?